VICTORYSERIES

STUDY 1

GOD'S
STORY
FOR YOU

DISCOVER THE PERSON
GOD CREATED YOU TO BE

NEIL T. ANDERSON

BETHANYHOUSE
a division of Baker Publishing Group
www.BethanyHouse.com

Published by Bethany House Publishers
11400 Hampshire Avenue South
Bloomington, Minnesota 55438
www.bethanyhouse.com

Bethany House Publishers is a division of
Baker Publishing Group, Grand Rapids, Michigan

Printed in the United States of America

Library of Congress Cataloging-in-Publication Data is on file at the Library of Congress, Washington, DC.

ISBN 978-0-7642-1367-0

Cover design by Inside Out Design

14   15   16   17   18   19   20   7   6   5   4   3   2   1

Contents

Contents

Introduction

The Victory Series

It's the beginning of another busy day. We want to look nice and make a good impression, so we spend some time showering, combing our hair, putting on makeup, and all the other grooming routines. Those who are more physically disciplined will find time to exercise. We have a quick bite to eat and it's off to work, school, or play.

Natural disciplines such as these are important. If we didn't do these things, we would suffer the consequences—whether that would be getting in trouble with our boss, or being tardy for school, or angering a friend because we didn't show up for an appointment. The same is true of spiritual disciplines, though it is easier for us to overlook their value, because we don't always see the immediate benefits. Wondering what's in it for us seems so unrighteous, but there are no sure commitments with no sure rewards.

The apostle Paul addresses this issue when he instructs us, "Train yourself to be godly. For physical training is of some value, but godliness has value for all things, holding promise for both the present life and the life to come" (1 Timothy 4:7–8). In other words, spiritual disciplines are more profitable than physical disciplines. Our lives will be more fruitful if we spend time with the Lord and seek to be transformed by the renewing of our minds to the truth of His Word.

What you are holding in your hands is the first study in the VICTORY SERIES on how you can discover God's story for you and uncover the person

He created you to be. As you work through the six sessions in this study, you will learn the story of God's creation, the effects of the Fall, God's plan for redemption, and how you can reconcile with God and become all He created you to be. You will discover who you are in Christ, what it means to be a child of God, and how to live a responsible and liberated life in Him. There are seven more studies in the VICTORY SERIES that will provide a practical systematic theology by which to live. All eight studies cover the subjects listed in the following tables.

As a believer in Christ, you must first be rooted "in Him" so you can be built up "in Him." Just as you encounter challenges as you grow physically, you will encounter hurdles as you grow spiritually. The following chart illustrates what obstacles you need to overcome and lessons you need to learn at various stages of growth spiritually, rationally, emotionally, volitionally, and relationally.

Levels of Conflict

	Level One Rooted in Christ	Level Two Built up in Christ	Level Three Living in Christ
Spiritual	Lack of salvation or assurance (Eph. 2:1–3)	Living according to the flesh (Gal. 5:19–21)	Insensitive to the Spirit's leading (Heb. 5:11–14)
Rational	Pride and ignorance (1 Cor. 8:1)	Wrong belief or philosophy (Col. 2:8)	Lack of knowledge (Hos. 4:6)
Emotional	Fearful, guilty, and shameful (Matt. 10:26–33; Rom. 3:23)	Angry, anxious, and depressed (Eph. 4:31; 1 Pet. 5:7; 2 Cor. 4:1–18)	Discouraged and sorrowful (Gal. 6:9)
Volitional	Rebellious (1 Tim. 1:9)	Lack of self-control (1 Cor. 3:1–3)	Undisciplined (2 Thess. 3:7, 11)
Relational	Rejected and unloved (1 Pet. 2:4)	Bitter and unforgiving (Col. 3:13)	Selfish (1 Cor. 10:24; Phil. 2:1–5)

This VICTORY SERIES will address these obstacles and hurdles and help you understand what it means to be firmly rooted in Christ, grow in Christ, live free in Christ, and overcome in Christ. The goal of the course is to help you attain greater levels of spiritual growth, as the following diagram illustrates:

Levels of Growth

	Level One Rooted in Christ	Level Two Built up in Christ	Level Three Living in Christ
Spiritual	Child of God (Rom. 8:16)	Lives according to the Spirit (Gal. 5:22–23)	Led by the Spirit (Rom. 8:14)
Rational	Knows the truth (John 8:32)	Correctly uses the Bible (2 Tim. 2:15)	Adequate and equipped (2 Tim. 3:16–17)
Emotional	Free (Gal. 5:1)	Joyful, peaceful, and patient (Gal. 5:22)	Contented (Phil. 4:11)
Volitional	Submissive (Rom. 13:1–5)	Self-controlled (Gal. 5:23)	Disciplined (1 Tim. 4:7–8)
Relational	Accepted and forgiven (Rom. 5:8; 15:7)	Forgiving (Eph. 4:32)	Loving and unselfish (Phil. 2:1–5)

Before starting each daily reading, review the portion of Scripture listed for that day, then complete the questions at the end of each day's reading. These questions have been written to allow you to reflect on the material and apply to your life the ideas presented in the reading. At the end of each study, I have included a quote from a Church father illustrating the continuity of the Christian faith. Featured articles will appear in the text throughout the series, which are for the edification of the reader and not necessarily meant for discussion.

If you are part of a small group, be prepared to share your thoughts and insights with your group. You may also want to set up an accountability partnership with someone in your group to encourage you as you apply what you have learned in each session. For those of you who are leading a small group, there are leader tips at the end of this book that will help you guide your participants through the material.

As with any spiritual discipline, you will be tempted at times not to finish this study. There is a "sure reward" for those who make a "sure commitment." The VICTORY SERIES is far more than an intellectual exercise. The truth will not set you free if you only acknowledge it and discuss it on an intellectual level. For the truth to transform your life, you must believe it personally and allow it to sink deep into your heart. Trust the Holy Spirit to lead you into all truth, and enable you to be the person God has created you to be. Decide to live what you have chosen to believe.

Dr. Neil T. Anderson

The Story of Creation

A long time ago, the infinite and eternal Creator sat down at His Potter's wheel as He had done so many times before. Everything He had made so far was very good, but this time He had something else in mind. He wanted to create something in His image. Something—or, better, some*one*—who could personally relate to Him. The Potter had already fashioned living beings to inhabit the earth, but this new creation would be different. Far more significant than all other earthen vessels, this new creation would be fruitful, and multiply, and rule over all the other created beings who flew in the sky, walked on the earth, or swam in the seas.

So He took a glob of clay and placed it on His wheel. As the wheel began to turn, He placed His thumbs in the center of the clay and formed the inward parts. Miraculously, the clay began to take shape. As the wheel turned faster and faster, the clay began to rise from the earth from which it was taken. Fearfully and wonderfully He made this new creation, which

He had planned from the beginning of time. But He wasn't done. Something was missing. The clay had no life. So He breathed into this earthen pot the breath of life and it became a living being. This fusion of divine life and earthly clay would make this new creation different from all other created beings. What appeared to be common was indeed holy, set apart to do His will.

Daily Readings

1. The Beginning	Genesis 1:1–31
2. The Nature of God	Psalm 19:1–14
3. The Nature of Humanity	Psalm 8:1–9
4. The Significance of Humanity	Genesis 2:1–25
5. The Way of Life	2 Samuel 22:1–51

1

The Beginning

Genesis 1:1–31

Key Point

The story of creation reveals the type of relationship we were supposed to have with our Creator and what our purpose is for being here.

Key Verse

For in him all things were created: things in heaven and on earth, visible and invisible, whether thrones or powers or rulers or authorities; all things have been created through him and for him.

Colossians 1:16

Every story has a beginning, a middle, and an end, and the Bible is no exception. The only difference is that with the Bible, the story starts at the *very* beginning—with the creation of the world. "In the beginning God created the heavens and the earth" (Genesis 1:1). These opening words reveal there is only one creator God who is eternally existent. In other words, while the story has a starting point, the One behind it does not. "I am the Alpha and the Omega—the beginning and the end," He says of Himself (Revelation 1:8). God has always been and always will be.

Throughout the Old Testament, the prophets acknowledged that God was the only source of all existence. "The LORD, the Maker of all things," Isaiah wrote, "stretches out the heavens . . . spreads out the earth by [Himself]" (44:24). The prophets understood that everything God made was completely dependent on Him for its survival. They also recognized that He alone was the sovereign Lord of the universe. Unlike the other people of their time, they never entertained the thought there could be more than one God.

Yet while the Bible makes it clear that God alone created the earth, nowhere are we told its exact age. This has led scholars to hold differing views on the subject. Some believe the world was created in seven literal days. Using the genealogy tables in Genesis as a guide, they propose a "young earth" theory that states the world has only been around for 10,000 to 20,000 years. Other scholars understand "day" to mean "age." They believe the earth to be much older—possibly millions of years older. However, whenever the Hebrew word "day" is used elsewhere in the Bible with a number (as it is throughout Genesis 1), it always refers to a 24-hour period of time.

Another possibility is that a gap of time exists between the first and second verses in Genesis. Genesis 1:2 reads, "The earth was formless and empty, darkness was over the surface of the deep, and the Spirit of God was hovering over the waters." Based on this theory, God could have created the earth thousands or millions of years before the events that occurred in the Garden of Eden. What we find in Genesis 1 would thus be a re-creation (or restoration) of the earth. This would account for the appearance of Satan in the Garden. God had previously created him, and he had subsequently rebelled and been cast out of heaven.

It is interesting to note that "in the beginning" literally means "by way of beginning." The creation narrative is therefore the starting point of history as we know it—but not necessarily the *absolute* start to creation. What the story does is set the stage for the creation of humanity and the unfolding drama of sin and redemption. It reveals the type of relationship that we were supposed to have with our Creator and what our purpose is for being here. Genesis 1–3, which depicts the creation of Adam and Eve and their subsequent fall, provides the backdrop that sets the stage for the rest of Scripture.

What do the opening words of the Bible reveal about God?

_____

_____

_____

What did the Old Testament prophets believe about God?

_____

_____

_____

Do the events in Genesis 1 depict the absolute beginning of creation? Why or why not?

_____

_____

_____

What does the creation account reveal about our intended relationship with God?

_____

_____

_____

How does knowing that God is sovereign and in control of His creation affect the way you conduct your life?

_____

_____

_____

The truth is, a great matter was in progress—out of which the creature under consideration was being fashioned. . . . Imagine God wholly employed and absorbed in it—in His hand, His eye, His labor, His purpose, His wisdom, His providence, and above all, in His love. All of these things were dictating the lineaments [of humanity]. For, whatever was the form and expression that was then given to the clay, it was in His thoughts that Christ would one day become man.

Tertullian (AD 160–220)

2

The Nature of God

Psalm 19:1–14

Key Point

God has revealed Himself as an integral part of our lives.

Key Verse

Since the creation of the world God's invisible qualities—his eternal power and divine nature—have been clearly seen, being understood from what has been made.

Romans 1:20

There comes a point in all stories where the main character—called the "protagonist"—is revealed. In the Bible, that protagonist is God, and He appears in the first sentence: "In the beginning God created the heavens and the earth" (Genesis 1:1). Throughout Scripture, we find that He continues to reveal Himself in three primary ways: (1) through general revelation, (2) through special revelation, and (3) through Christ.

"General revelation" refers to the way God reveals Himself through the beauty and order of His creation. David proclaims, "The heavens declare the glory of God; the skies proclaim the work of his hands" (Psalm 19:1). "Special revelation" refers to the way God reveals Himself through the divinely inspired prophets and apostles who wrote the books of the Bible. In the written Word, God defines Himself and explains who we are and why we are here. However, Jesus is the ultimate revelation of God. Jesus declared, "Anyone who has seen me has seen the Father" (John 14:9).

The Bible never portrays God as some impersonal deity who creates the world and then walks away. In fact, we find that He is integral to every aspect of His creation. His Word speaks to matters of faith as well as matters of everyday practice; to the spiritual and sacred as well as to the physical and secular; and to the eternal as well as the temporal. The Bible addresses every essential discipline in society.

For example, "in the beginning God created the heavens and the earth" (Genesis 1:1) is laden with theological and philosophical ramifications. God planting "the tree of the knowledge of good and evil" (Genesis 2:9) in the Garden of Eden speaks to ethics, and creating the animal kingdom "according to their kinds" (Genesis 1:21) speaks to biological distinctions. The statement that "man became a living being" (Genesis 2:7) addresses humans' psychological, spiritual, and physical nature. God's command to "be fruitful and increase in number" (Genesis 1:28) is a sociological and ecological statement, and He speaks to political and legal concerns when He says, "Whoever sheds the blood of man, by man shall his blood be shed" (Genesis 9:6). His words to Adam and Eve that every seed-bearing plant "will be yours for food" (Genesis 1:29) is an economic statement. His statement, "I will put enmity between you and the woman" (Genesis 3:15), contains historical and prophetic ramifications.

God underlines the significance of all these disciplines in the ultimate revelation of Jesus Christ. In theology and philosophy, Jesus is the fullness of the Godhead (see Colossians 2:9) and the *Logos* (Word) of God (see John 1:1). In ethics, Jesus is the true light (see John 1:9). In biology, He took on the form of a man (see Philippians 2:7) and became our source for physical and spiritual life (see John 1:4). In psychology, Jesus is the true and perfect man who saves and transforms us (see Luke 1:46–47). In sociology, Jesus is our example for social relationships (see 1 Peter 2:21). In law and politics, Jesus came to fulfill the Law (see Matthew 5:17) and is the King of kings (see Revelation 19:16). In economics, Jesus is the owner of all things (see 1 Corinthians 10:26). In history and prophecy, Jesus is the beginning and the end (see Revelation 1:8).

In what three primary ways has God chosen to reveal Himself to humans?

_____

_____

_____

What evidence do we have from Scripture that God desires to be intimately involved in the lives of His people?

_____

_____

_____

Read Psalm 19:7–11. What appreciation does David express to God for giving laws and for guiding his steps?

_____

_____

_____

What comfort can you take in knowing that God is integral to every part of your life? How does it make you feel to understand that He wants you to know Him?

_____

_____

_____

In what ways has God personally made Himself known to you?

_____

_____

_____

We bring under your notice something of even greater importance; we point to the majesty of our Scriptures, if not to their antiquity. If you doubt that they are as ancient as we say, we offer proof that they are divine. . . . For all that is taking place around you was foretold. All that you now see with your eyes was previously heard by the ear: the swallowing up of cities by the earth; the theft of islands by the sea; wars, bringing external and internal convulsions; famines and pestilences. . . . It was all foreseen and predicted before it came to pass. While we suffer the calamities, we read of them in the Scriptures. They are written in the same books, for the same Spirit inspires them.

Tertullian (AD 160–220)

3

The Nature of Humanity

Psalm 8:1–9

Key Point

We were created to be both physically and spiritually alive.

Key Verse

God created man in his own image, in the image of God he created them; male and female he created them.

Genesis 1:27

In the beginning of God's story, we read that He created the heavens and the earth, day and night, water and sky, plants and trees, and all forms of animal life. Then God "created mankind in his own image, in the image of God he created them" (Genesis 1:27). He set humans apart from the animal kingdom and gave them the ability to think, feel, and choose. As a result, humans have the unique ability to participate with God in the shaping of their lives. Such an act caused David to ponder, "What is mankind that you are mindful of them, human beings that you care for them?" (Psalm 8:4).

A bit further into the creation story, we find that God "formed the man from the dust of the ground and breathed into his nostrils the breath of life, and the man became a living being" (Genesis 2:7). This combination of the "dust of the ground" (the natural) and the "breath of life" (the spiritual) is what constitutes the nature of humanity. The original creation of man could be depicted as follows:

Body/Heart

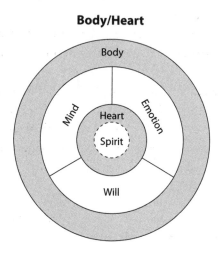

Some believe humans are composed of body, soul, and spirit (trichotomous) and that the mind, will, and emotion constitute the soul. Others understand the human soul and spirit to be essentially the same (dichotomous). Most would agree that part of our human existence is material and part is immaterial—that each of us possesses an inner person and an outer person. As Paul writes, "Even though our outward man is perishing, yet the inward man is being renewed day by day" (2 Corinthians 4:16 NKJV).

God created Adam to be both physically and spiritually alive. He was "physically" alive in that his soul/spirit was united with his body—and he would remain physically alive as long as his soul remained in union with his body. He was "spiritually" alive in that his soul/spirit was in union with God. When Christians die physically, they are absent from their bodies but spiritually present with the Lord. Paul states, "We are always confident, knowing that while we are at home in the body we are absent from the Lord" (2 Corinthians 5:6 NKJV).

We have a physical body that enables us to relate to the natural world through our five senses. Consequently, we can taste, smell, feel, hear, and see. Our minds, wills, and emotions come together in the heart, which forms the core of our inner being. "As in water face reflects face, so a man's heart reveals the man" (Proverbs 27:19 NKJV). We are not the source of our life, so our hearts are inherently open to external influences. What we take into our hearts becomes its master, stamping our hearts with its character.

In the original creation, God was at the center of Adam's and Eve's lives, and they naturally took on His character. They were created to be a little lower than heavenly beings, crowned with glory and honor, and given dominion over the animal kingdom (see Psalm 8:5–6). They were dependent creatures who acknowledged God as the creator and sustainer of life.

According to Psalm 8:5–8, what position do human beings have in relation to everything else that God created?

_____

_____

_____

What does it mean to be "physically alive"? What does it mean to be "spiritually alive"?

_____

_____

_____

_____

In what ways do each of us possess an "inner person" and an "outer person"?

_____

_____

_____

What have you taken into your heart (greed, selfish ambition, lust, pride, chemicals), thus supplanting God as the central force in your life?

_____

_____

_____

How can you take on the character of Christ?

_____

_____

_____

When all things had been settled with a wonderful arrangement, He determined to prepare for Himself an eternal kingdom and to create innumerable souls, on whom He might bestow immortality. Then He made for Himself a figure endowed with perception and intelligence—that is, after the likeness of His own image. . . . So He formed man out of the dust of the ground.

Lactantius (AD 240–320)

4

The Significance of Humanity

Genesis 2:1–25

Key Point

In union with God we are safe, secure, significant, and endowed with a divine purpose for being here.

Key Verse

So we fix our eyes not on what is seen, but on what is unseen, since what is seen is temporary, but what is unseen is eternal.

2 Corinthians 4:18

The setting in which the story of humanity began is one of beauty, peace, and tranquility. Adam lived in the presence of God in the Garden of Eden, and God met all of his physical needs as well as his psychological needs for acceptance, security, and significance. Adam was significant because God had created him in His own image and likeness. He had also given Adam a divine purpose: "Rule over the fish in the sea and the birds in the sky and over every living creature that moves on the ground" (Genesis 1:28).

Adam's first assignment was to tend the Garden of Eden (see Genesis 2:15), and his first act of taking dominion over the creatures was to name them (see verse 20). At that time Satan was not the "ruler of this world" (John 12:31 NASB) or the "god of this age" (2 Corinthians 4:4), nor did he have any claim over the earth. God had given that responsibility solely to Adam and his descendants.

God's story tells us that the tree of life was in the center of the Garden of Eden. Adam could freely eat from it and from any tree of the Garden. The only restriction the Lord gave to him was that he could not eat from the tree of the knowledge of good and evil (see Genesis 2:15–17). Had Adam chosen to obey God and continue to depend on God to meet all his needs, he would have lived forever.

God saw that all He had made was "very good" (Genesis 1:31), except for one thing—it was not good "for the man to be alone" (2:18). So God created a "helper suitable for him" (verse 18). She and Adam were naked and unashamed (see verse 25). There was no sin in their lives, and they had nothing to hide. Adam and Eve could have an intimate sexual relationship in the presence of God. They were unconditionally loved and accepted and had a sense of belonging to God and to each another. They were both physically and psychologically secure in the presence of God.

The Lord gave Adam and Eve an assignment: "Be fruitful and increase in number; fill the earth and subdue it" (Genesis 1:28). God had created humans in His own image, and it was His intention for Adam and Eve to form a culture that would bear the image of their Creator and participate as servants in His kingly rule. The birds of the sky, the beasts of the field, and the fish of the sea all operated according to instinct, but God had given humans the ability to think, feel, and choose. No other creature had been given this gift or been assigned such significance on earth.

Each of us is a reflection of our Creator. Our existence has meaning, and we maintain that significance as long as we stay intimately connected to the source of all life. As Paul writes, "We fix our eyes not on what is seen, but on what is unseen" (2 Corinthians 4:18). Our faith in the invisible God is the only means by which we can withstand the seductive powers of the visible world.

Why was Adam significant? What assignment did God give to him?

How does the sense of safety, significance, and security that was evident in the Garden differ from what we see in the world today? What changed?

What was the purpose for humanity, whom God had created in His image and likeness?

What does it mean to you to fix your eyes "not on what is seen, but on what is unseen"?

Do you personally feel safe? Secure? Significant? Why or why not?

God designed the world for the sake of man. But He formed man for Himself for His own sake. Man was, as it were, a priest of a divine temple, a spectator of God's works and of heavenly objects. For he is the only [earthly] being who is able to understand God, for he is intelligent and capable of reason. . . . On this account, he alone of all the other living creatures has been made with an upright body and stance. So it seems that he is raised up for the contemplation of his Parent. For this reason also, he alone has received language . . . so that he may be able to declare the majesty of his Lord. . . . So it is plainly most just that man should worship Him who bestowed such great gifts upon him. He should also love his fellow man, who is united with him in the participation of the divine justice.

Lactantius (AD 240–320)

5

The Way of Life

2 Samuel 22:1–51

Key Point

God created us to live in a certain way that is pleasing to Him and fulfilling for us.

Key Verse

I am the way and the truth and the life. No one comes to the Father except through me.

John 14:6

The story of creation as told in Genesis 1–3 reveals that God designed humanity to live in a certain way and that His way was perfect (see 2 Samuel 22:31). God had intended for His children to draw on His strength and receive power to live the way He had designed for them to live. David understood this concept when he wrote, "It is God who arms me with strength and keeps my way secure" (verse 33). Later, in the days of the Early Church, believers in Christ would say that they "belonged to the Way" (Acts 9:2). They knew that Jesus was the *only way* to God (see John 14:6).

29

Every object that humans have created has been designed to function in only one way. A computer can perform many functions, but it has to be used the way the manufacturer intended. If you have never read the manufacturer's instruction book, there isn't much you can do with a computer. If you ignore the instructions and decide to use the computer the way you want, it will be a worthless tool. However, if you mastered the instruction book, the computer can perform incredible functions. Likewise, we have been designed to live in a certain way as revealed by the Creator's instruction book. Little knowledge of the Bible results in limited potential of fulfilling our destiny.

We will be tempted to live in other ways relying on our own strength and resources. We will be tempted to lean on our own understanding instead of in all ways acknowledging God, thinking that we know what is best for our own lives. In our pride, we may even deceive ourselves into thinking we don't need the help of God and others. All of these ways will seem right to us, but in the end they only lead to death (see Proverbs 16:25).

We may also be tempted to question God's wisdom in creating us the way we are and for not giving us more favorable circumstances in which to live. This is much like a piece of pottery questioning the way it was made and the purpose the creator had in making it. As Paul states, "Who are you, a human being, to talk back to God? 'Shall what is formed say to the one who formed it, "Why did you make me like this?"' Does not the potter have the right to make out of the same lump of clay some pottery for special purposes and some for common use?" (Romans 9:20–21).

The key for successful living is to know God, learn His ways, and then live accordingly by faith in the power of the Holy Spirit. The Bible is clear that we are not to live in our own strength but only in the power of the Holy Spirit. Paul wrote, "Let the one who boasts boast in the Lord" (1 Corinthians 1:31). As humans created in God's image, we will only fulfill our purpose when we follow the path that our Creator has designed for us—when we "boast" in God's wisdom and strength, and not our own.

In David's song of praise to God, he wrote, "I have kept the ways of the LORD; I have not done evil by turning from my God" (2 Samuel 22:22). What a world this would be if all God's creation could say the same.

To what did David attribute his success over his enemies in 2 Samuel 22:21–25?

How is personal rebellion in conflict with "the way"? What is the basis for people making that choice?

How is personal pride in complete contrast with boasting in the Lord?

What inner conflicts do you sense when confronted with the choice of living God's way or your way?

What external forces or temptations are likely to draw you away from knowing and living God's way?

We understand the "way" to be the road to perfection, advancing in order step by step through the words of righteousness and the illumination of knowledge, always yearning for that which lies ahead and straining toward the last mile, until we reach that blessed end, the knowledge of God, with which the Lord blesses those who believe in Him. For truly our Lord is a good way, a straight road with no confusing forks or turns, leading us directly to the Father. For "no one comes to the Father," He says, "except through Me." Such is our way up to God through His Son.

Basil the Great (AD 330–379)

The Story of the Fall

All would have been well for the newly formed pots if it hadn't been for a previously created being who thought he should be at least equal to the Potter. That, of course, was an absurd notion, even though he was the most beautiful of all created things. This masterpiece was created to be a light-bearer. However, by his own choice, this rebel became the prince of darkness. Not wanting to be alone in his rebellion, this arrogant spirit persuaded many other lesser spirits to join him. The Potter could not tolerate this sinful rebellion. So He cast the spirits out of His presence, and they fell from their heavenly abode.

The prince of darkness could not stand the thought that a new creation by the Potter would actually rule over him. If only he could get this new creation to act independently of the Potter. *I know what I shall do*, thought the evil prince. *I'll get this upstart pot to think that he too could be like the Potter and decide for himself what is good and evil.* This crafty devil actually managed to deceive this new creation by questioning the word of the Potter, enticing him to do his own thing and live independently of the One who fashioned him. The consequences were swift and immediate. The Divine breath departed and impurities were introduced into the clay.

Daily Readings

1. The Challenge in the Garden	Genesis 3:1–24
2. The Deception of Eve	1 Timothy 2:11–15
3. The Sin of Adam	Ezekiel 3:16–19
4. The Effects of the Fall	Genesis 4:1–26
5. Meaningless Living	Ecclesiastes 1:1–18

1

The Challenge in the Garden
Genesis 3:1–24

Key Point

Satan's main goal is to tempt us to live independently of God.

Key Verse

Consequently, just as the result of one trespass was condemnation for all men, so also the result of one act of righteousness was justification that brings life for all men.

Romans 5:18

God, the protagonist of His story, created the world and everything in it. He fashioned Adam and Eve in His own image and gave them a perfect place to live. They wanted for nothing, for He provided for all of their needs. But it wasn't long before the enemy of God—the "antagonist" in our story—slithered into the Garden to challenge Adam and Eve's God-given dominion over the earth.

Throughout Church history, the serpent has been identified as Satan—or at least a beast possessed by Satan. The New Testament writers referred to Satan as "the tempter" and "the father of lies" (see Matthew 4:3; John 8:44). Later, the apostle John would clearly identify Satan, the one who leads the whole world astray, as "that ancient serpent called the devil" (Revelation 12:9).

Satan's first target was Eve, and his tactic was to cause her to question God's Word. He asked, "Did God really say, 'You must not eat from any tree in the garden'?" (Genesis 3:1). Eve responded, "We may eat from the trees in the garden, but God did say, 'You must not eat fruit from the tree that is in the middle of the garden, and you must *not touch it*, or you will die'" (verse 3, emphasis added). Immediately Satan challenged her. "You will not surely die . . . for God knows that when you eat of it your eyes will be opened, and you will be like God, knowing good and evil" (verses 4–5).

Did you catch what Eve added to God's word? Such is the subtlety of deception. To have knowledge of good and evil means to be the one who determines what is good and evil or what is true or untrue. Thus, when Adam and Eve chose to eat the forbidden fruit, they were in effect saying, "We reject the notion that God is the only one who determines what is right or wrong. We will determine for ourselves what is good for us." In a distorted way, Satan was right—by choosing to believe it was their prerogative to determine what was right and wrong, they would be acting like gods.

The immediate consequence of Adam and Eve's rebellion was spiritual death, for their souls were no longer in union with God. The Lord banished them from the Garden of Eden (see verse 23), and because they no longer had access to the tree of life, physical death would soon follow. Every descendant of Adam and Eve from that day forward would be born physically alive but spiritually dead (see Ephesians 2:1). They would have neither the presence of God in their lives nor the knowledge of His ways. In addition, Adam and Eve forfeited their right to rule and allowed Satan to become the rebel holder of authority in this world (see John 16:11; 2 Corinthians 4:4).

Satan thought he had thwarted God's plan, but the Lord responded by promising that one day a future descendant of Eve would crush him: "I will put enmity between you and the woman, and between your offspring and hers; he will crush your head, and you will strike his heel" (Genesis

3:15). Satan would inflict damage on the people of God, but the seed of the woman would strike the fatal blow by crushing the serpent's head. This promise would be fulfilled in Christ's victory over Satan.

Read Genesis 3:1–7. In what ways were Adam and Eve's "eyes opened" after they disobeyed God and sinned?

Why do you think Satan was able to tempt Eve by promising she would be like God? How does he tempt people today with the same false promise?

What were the immediate and lasting consequences of Adam and Eve's rebellion? How does that affect us today?

Considering what Adam and Eve lost during the Fall, what would Jesus have to do in order to save humanity?

Since the devil is still roaring around like a hungry lion, how can you protect yourself from being deceived?

_____

_____

_____

That deception was done away with, by which that virgin Eve (who was already espoused to a man) was unhappily misled. [Its overturning] was happily announced by means of the truth through the angel to the Virgin Mary, who was [espoused] to a man. . . . And if Eve did disobey God, yet Mary was persuaded to be obedient to God. This was in order that the Virgin Mary might become the advocate of the virgin Eve. And thus, as the human race fell into bondage to death by means of a virgin, so is it rescued by a virgin.

Irenaeus (AD 130–202)

2

The Deception of Eve

1 Timothy 2:11–15

Key Point

Being submissive does not imply inferiority.

Key Verse

Two are better than one, because they have a good return for their labor.

Ecclesiastes 4:9

When God began to write the story of our earth—scripting into place the heavens, the land, the seas, the vegetation, and the animal life—he did not include humans with the rest of creation. The Lord created Adam later and placed him in the Garden of Eden to work it and care for it. After this, he formed Eve from a part of the man. Adam knew the difference immediately and proclaimed, "This is now bone of my bones and flesh of my flesh" (Genesis 2:23).

God's story from the beginning was perfect, and His plan was never for the man and woman to be in competition with one another. Adam was honored in knowing that God had created Eve for him, and she was honored in knowing that Adam was incomplete without her. Eve came into being through the power of God, from man, and she was to be "a helper suitable for him" (Genesis 2:18). God intended Eve to have a complementary relationship with Adam.

The fact that Satan could deceive Eve and entice her to believe a lie is a sobering reality of life. Satan's major tool is deception, and he uses it to lead good people—even innocent people—away from God. His ability to convince Eve that something was true when it was not led to swift judgment from the Lord: "I will make your pains in childbearing very severe; with painful labor you will give birth to children. Your desire will be for your husband, and he will rule over you" (Genesis 3:16).

Any mother could testify to the first part of the curse being true. The second part has been far harder for us to work out in our homes, churches, and societies. We witness this challenge when we read verses such as 1 Timothy 2:12, where Paul instructs, "I do not permit a woman to teach or to assume authority over a man; she must be quiet." The issue at stake is one of authority, not inferiority, or the stifling of a woman's contribution to the Church. God has given abilities and talents to everyone regardless of gender, and every child of God should use his or her gifts to the glory of God.

Paul's admonition that he does not permit a woman to teach refers more to the establishment of doctrine rather than proclaiming the truth in love (see Ephesians 4:15). In making this instruction to the Church, Paul was following the order for spiritual authority that God had established at the time of creation. Sadly, many congregations over the centuries have taken his words to the extreme, causing undue hardship to the women of this world and prohibiting them from making valuable contributions to the Church and society. To the other extreme, women have rebelled against this instruction, resulting in the Word of God being dishonored (see Titus 2:5).

When God established spiritual authority, He did so for the protection and benefit of His creation. Being submissive does not imply inferiority, for the image of God is as equally present in women as it is in men.

Wherever Christianity has flourished, women have been afforded equal status with men.

What is keeping male and female relationships from being complementary instead of competitive?

_____

_____

_____

What curse did God give to Eve as a result of her rebellion? How has that played out in our churches?

_____

_____

_____

In light of the curse, how can ministries be shaped such that both men and women can have the fullest potential to use their gifts and talents to the glory of God?

_____

_____

_____

What has shaped your perception of the opposite gender? How has that affected the way you relate to them?

_____

_____

_____

Christianity has afforded greater status to women more than any other religion in the world, but in some cases not always equal. Why do you think that is? Why have women been so dominated by men in the pagan world?

_____

_____

_____

God formed Eve into a wife from out of his rib. . . . He did this lest it would be supposed that one God made the man and another God made the woman. Therefore, He made them both. And God made the woman together with the man, not only so that thereby the mystery of God's sole government might be displayed, but also so that their mutual love might be greater.

Theophilus (died c. AD 181)

3

The Sin of Adam

Ezekiel 3:16–19

Key Point

We can choose to live dependently on or independently of God, and both choices have sure consequences.

Key Verse

For as in Adam all die, so in Christ all will be made alive.

1 Corinthians 15:22

E ve was deceived, but Adam willfully sinned against the Lord. Adam knew what he was doing and made a *conscious choice* to disobey his Creator. As a result of his actions, "Sin entered the world through one man, and death through sin, and in this way death came to all men, because all sinned" (Romans 5:12). The Bible clearly tells us that "the wages of sin is death" (Romans 6:23). Sin separates us from a holy God, which is spiritual death; and because we no longer have His life to sustain us, it also leads to physical death. Each of us is destined to die once, and after that we will face judgment (see Hebrews 9:27).

43

God had clearly warned Adam that he would die if he disobeyed Him, but Adam did not remain alert to the dangers of sin. Centuries later, the people would station watchmen at the highest parts of the city to warn the inhabitants of coming danger. God told prophets such as Ezekiel that they were to serve as spiritual watchmen, warning the people that He would hold them accountable for not keeping His law. He said, "When I say to a wicked person, 'You will surely die,' and you do not warn them or speak out to dissuade them from their evil ways . . . I will hold you accountable for their blood" (Ezekiel 3:18).

In order to understand holiness, we must first understand sin. However, this is difficult for us to grasp because we all have sinned and live in an environment affected by sin. Other than Christ, nobody has ever experienced perfect holiness, so it is hard for us to discern the difference between society's norms and genuine righteousness. We are continually exposed to sin and learn to tolerate it, which causes our awareness of what is truly sinful to grow dull. Furthermore, none of us has experienced the full weight of the consequences for our sins. If we had, we might choose a different course.

Satan did not *make* Adam sin. God had created Adam in His image and given him the capacity to choose whether or not to obey His commands. Adam failed to keep watch and sinned of his own free will, and for this reason he became responsible for the presence and consequences of sin in the world. We, like Adam, have also sinned, and we must bear the consequences of that sin. Spiritual death silences every attempt we might make to transfer, even partially, our guilt to Satan, by whom man was first tempted.

God has authentic freedom and cannot sin, and He created Adam and Eve with a freedom that was dependent on Him. The concept of freedom lies at the very heart of God. As long as Adam and Eve refrained from sin, they could freely live. Disobedience results in bondage to sin. Freedom is more than the exercise of choice; it is always related to the consequences of that choice. Paul wrote, "Everything that does not come from faith is sin" (Romans 14:23). Adam and Eve ultimately lost their freedom and their lives because of the lies they believed and the sin they willfully committed. Thankfully, neither sin nor death has the final word.

Read Genesis 3:6–7. Why did Adam choose to sin?

How can we be deceived into thinking that we are living a righteous life when in reality we aren't?

What does it mean that "everything that does not come from faith is sin?"

How can we train ourselves to consider the short-term and long-term consequences of our choices?

What will be the impact on society when nobody has to suffer the consequences of poor choices, and how will that affect their path toward maturity?

The Lord came to the lost sheep. He made a recapitulation of a very comprehensive dispensation, and He sought after His own handiwork. Therefore, it was necessary for Him to save the very man who had been created after His image and likeness—that is, Adam. . . . Man had been created by God to live. However, he was injured by the serpent who had corrupted him. Now, if after losing life, and would never again return to life (but would be utterly abandoned to death), then God would have been conquered. The wickedness of the serpent would have prevailed over the will of God.

Irenaeus (AD 130–202)

4

The Effects of the Fall

Genesis 4:1–26

Key Point

Apart from God we are darkened in our understanding and riddled with fear, anxiety, and depression.

Key Verse

The person without the Spirit does not accept the things that come from the Spirit of God but considers them foolishness, and cannot understand them because they are discerned only through the Spirit.

1 Corinthians 2:14

Sin had separated Adam and Eve from God. Their spiritual death had immediate and dramatic effects on their ability to think, feel, and choose. Even their knowledge of God was distorted, which became evident when Adam and Eve tried to hide from an omnipresent and omniscient God (see Genesis 3:7–8). They were "darkened in their understanding and separated from the life of God" (Ephesians 4:18), which is true of all

47

those who have no relationship with Him. Lacking the presence of God they had no spiritual discernment (see 1 Corinthians 2:14).

Adam and Eve were also emotionally distraught and became fearful and anxious. The first emotion that Adam expressed was fear (see Genesis 3:10). "Fear not" became the most repeated commandment after the Fall, occurring 400 times in Scripture. To this day, anxiety disorders are the number one mental health problem of the world.

Before the Fall Adam and Eve had been naked and unashamed, but now they were filled with guilt and shame. They wanted to hide and cover up, as many do today. They wear a mask, fearing that others will find out what is really going on inside them.

Adam and Eve's descendants suffered the effects of their parents' sin and were also plagued by anger and depression. Cain brought his offering to God, but God wasn't pleased with it, and he became angry. The Lord said to him, "Why are you angry? Why is your face downcast? If you do what is right, will you not be accepted? But if you do not do what is right, sin is crouching at your door; it desires to have you, but you must rule over it" (Genesis 4:6–7). In other words, we don't *feel* our way into good behavior; we *behave* our way into good feeling.

Before the Fall, Adam and Eve had been faced with only one bad choice. Afterward, they were plagued by choices every moment of every day. The same is true for us. Apart from God's presence in our lives, the greatest power we possess is the ability to make choices. We can choose to pray or not pray. We can choose to believe or not believe.

Before the Fall, Adam and Eve were unconditionally accepted and had a sense of belonging to God and each other. Now they were confronted with feelings of rejection. Every lost soul struggles with the need to belong. We will never fully overcome the power of peer pressure and the fear of rejection until our legitimate need to belong is met in Christ.

The loss of Adam and Eve's innocence created an identity crisis and led them on a search for significance. The loss of their spiritual life left them weak and helpless. Separated from God, they had no choice but to seek their identity in the natural order of this fallen world, find their purpose and meaning in life independent of God, and try to meet their needs through their own strength and resources.

For Adam and Eve, there was only one thing that changed from the tranquility of the Garden to mental and emotional depravity—they died spiritually. What must happen if we want to resolve mental and emotional problems today?

_____

_____

_____

_____

Why do so many people suffer from an identity crisis and a low sense of worth?

_____

_____

_____

How does the world tell us to find acceptance, security, and significance?

_____

_____

_____

What Adam and Eve possessed as attributes before the Fall became glaring needs after the Fall. How can these needs be met in our lives?

_____

_____

_____

Do you believe that new life in Christ has the possibility of meeting those needs in your life? Why or why not?

_____

_____

_____

God ordained that, if man kept this, he would partake of immortal existence. However, if he transgressed it, his lot would be just the opposite. Having been made in this manner, man soon went toward transgression. And so he naturally became subject to corruption. Therefore, corruption became inherent in nature. So it was necessary that He who wished to save us would be someone who destroyed the essential cause of corruption. . . . For if, as you suggest, He had simply warded off death from us by a simple nod, indeed death would not have approached us—on account of His will. However, we would have again become corruptible, for we carried about in ourselves that natural corruption.

Justin Martyr (AD 100–165)

5

Meaningless Living

Ecclesiastes 1:1–18

Key Point

We are incomplete without Christ, and nothing we can do through our human efforts will make us whole.

Key Verses

The creation was subjected to frustration, not by its own choice, but by the will of the one who subjected it, in hope that the creation itself will be liberated from its bondage to decay and brought into the freedom and glory of the children of God.

Romans 8:20–21

God's story for Adam and Eve—and for all of humanity—was not yet over. As we have seen, even as He was issuing the curse against the serpent, He was looking toward the time when Christ would ultimately crush Satan's head (see Genesis 3:15). In the meantime, Adam and Eve had lost their relationship with God, and now they and all their descendants had little choice but to try to meet their own needs in a fallen world. Even though God's plan for redemption was slowly unfolding, they had to struggle to find purpose and meaning in life without an intimate relationship with God.

Solomon understood the challenge of this struggle. As king of Israel during the time the nation enjoyed its greatest prominence, he had the ability to do almost anything he wanted. He had accumulated great wealth and military strength (see 1 Kings 10:14–29). God had given him more wisdom than any other human to interpret his findings and observations (see 1 Kings 3:12). If anyone on earth could have possibly met his or her own personal needs, Solomon had the best chance.

Yet even with all these riches and power at his disposal, Solomon could find no purpose and meaning in life while living independently of God. "Meaningless! Meaningless!" he declared in the book of Ecclesiastes. "Utterly meaningless! Everything is meaningless. . . . I have seen all the things that are done under the sun; all of them are meaningless, a chasing after the wind" (Ecclesiastes 1:2, 14).

Today, we still struggle with our own personal identity and our reason for being here. When God issued the curse against Adam and Eve, He stated that women would bear their children in pain and men would work by the sweat of their brow (see Genesis 3:16–19). Consequently, women have historically tried to find their identity in their role as mothers, while men have tried to find their identity in their careers. But what if a woman never gets married or is unable to bear children? What if a man loses his job or his ability to work? Do those men and women lose their primary identity in Christ and their God-given purpose for being here?

Acting as our own god, we strive to make a name for ourselves. We search for significance by improving our appearance, performing better, and seeking a higher social status. However, like Solomon, we soon find that whatever pinnacle of self-identity we reach crumbles under the pressure of rejection, criticism, morbid introspection, guilt, fear, and shame. There is always someone who looks better, performs at a higher standard, and reaches a higher social status. We are faced with the realization that everything we have sought to possess through our human efforts will one day pass away. We are incomplete without Christ, and nothing we can do by way of self-effort will make us whole.

We all have a longing for wholeness and feel the sting of its absence. In this we are not alone, for as Paul writes, "We know that the whole creation has been groaning as in the pains of childbirth right up to the present time" (Romans 8:22). All of creation in God's story was affected by the Fall and longs for the day of redemption.

Do you think the average person feels good about himself or herself? Why or why not?

_____

_____

_____

Can a natural person find his or her identity and develop a good sense of worth by being attractive, or by performing better, or by having social status? Why or why not?

_____

_____

_____

Are there any insignificant children of God? Explain your answer.

_____

_____

_____

Who are you (not your name), and how do you feel about yourself?

_____

_____

_____

Before we look at the gospel in the next section, ask several people a simple question: "Who are you?" If they share their name, say, "That is just your name. *Who* are you?" Write down the different responses that you hear.

_____

_____

_____

The corruption of our nature is another nature having a god and father of its own—namely, the author of corruption. Still, there is a portion of good in the soul, of that original, divine, and genuine good, which is its proper nature. For that which is derived from God is obscured, rather than extinguished. It can indeed be obscured, because it is not God. However, it cannot be extinguished, for it comes from God. . . . Thus some men are very bad, and some are very good. Yet, the souls of everyone are all of one nature. Even in the worst person, there is something good. And even in the best person, there is something bad. . . . Just as no soul is without sin, so neither is any soul without seeds of good.

Tertullian (AD 160–220)

The Story of Salvation

The Potter had designed His pots to multiply and fill the earth, but all their offspring had similar impurities and were separated from the Potter. They had lost dominion over other living beings, and the prince of darkness became the rebel holder of authority, the god of this world, and the prince of the power of the air. But the Potter loved what He had molded and had a plan to undo the works of this rebel prince—a plan that would remove the impurities that now characterized all His creation. This plan would also restore His life in the hopeless and helpless pots.

The Potter's plan required Himself to take on the form of a pot and show the earthy pots how to live by faith in His power. The prince of darkness threw every temptation at this Divine Pot, hoping that He too would choose to live independently of the Potter. But He came to do far more than show us how to live, because the pots still lacked life, and the consequences of impurities was certain destruction. So the Divine Pot took upon Himself all the consequences of the impurities of the fallen pots, and the natural life of the Divine Pot was extinguished, but justice was served. He died once for all the fallen pots who would trust in Him.

Then, three days later, the Divine Pot was resurrected, showing that His natural death had defeated the prince of darkness, and made it possible for all the fallen pots to be forgiven and receive divine life.

Daily Readings

1. The Good News	Philemon 1:1–25
2. Forgiveness of Sins	Hebrews 9:11–28
3. New Life in Christ	John 6:25–59
4. New Identity in Christ	John 1:1–14
5. The Defeat of Satan	1 John 3:7–15

1

The Good News

Philemon 1:1–25

Key Point

The whole gospel can be summarized by Jesus' coming to die for our sins, give us eternal life, and undo the works of Satan.

Key Verse

I am the resurrection and the life. He who believes in me will live [spiritually], even though he dies [physically].

John 11:25

The apostle Paul's letter to Philemon portrays his passion for the gospel, and he is a testimony of those who believe it. Paul had been imprisoned in Rome for preaching the gospel. Onesimus was a recipient of his preaching and gladly received this "good news." His life was transformed. Onesimus was useless before Paul shared the gospel with him, but now he was useful to Paul and Philemon (see verse 11). Before he was a slave, but now he was a brother in Christ. His identity and character changed.

Paul prays that every believer would share this good news of salvation in Christ and that they would fully understand all that they have in Him (see verse 6). To understand the gospel, one has to understand the plight of fallen humanity, which the apostle Paul summarizes in Ephesians 2:1–2: "As for you, you were dead in your transgressions and sins, in which you used to live when you followed the ways of this world and of the ruler of the kingdom of the air."

To overcome the effects of the Fall, three primary issues would have to be resolved. First, the sin that separates humanity from a holy God had to be atoned for. "For all have sinned and fall short of the glory of God, and all are justified freely by his grace through the redemption that came by Christ Jesus" (Romans 3:23–24). Jesus died for our sins in order that we may be forgiven.

Second, it is not enough that our sins are forgiven if we are still spiritually dead. To save people who have already died, we would have to first cure the disease that caused them to die. Because of Christ's death on the cross we are forgiven, and because of His resurrection we have eternal life. "For the wages of sin is death, but the gift of God is eternal life in Christ Jesus our Lord" (Romans 6:23). What Adam and Eve lost was spiritual life, and Jesus came to give us life (see John 10:10). As children of God we have received a glorious inheritance in Christ (see Ephesians 1:18) and have become new creations in Christ (see 2 Corinthians 5:17).

Paul wrote, "Now, brothers and sisters, I want to remind you of the gospel I preached to you. . . . If there is no resurrection of the dead, then not even Christ has been raised. And if Christ has not been raised, our preaching is useless and so is your faith" (1 Corinthians 15:1, 13–14). Because of the resurrection, we have new life in Christ, and that eternal life is not something we get when we die physically. We receive eternal life the moment we are born again. "Whoever has the Son has life; whoever does not have the Son of God does not have life" (1 John 5:12). Jesus said, "I am the resurrection and the life. He who believes in me will live, even though he dies" (John 11:25). In other words, those who believe in Jesus will continue to live spiritually even when they die physically.

Third, "The reason the Son of God appeared was to destroy the devil's work" (1 John 3:8). Jesus defeated the devil and disarmed him (see

Colossians 2:15), and we are no longer subject to him because every believer is now seated with Christ in the heavenlies (see Ephesians 2:6).

Read Colossians 2:13–15. What are the three primary aspects of the gospel?

_____

_____

_____

_____

Which of those three aspects of the gospel are most overlooked in our churches today?

_____

_____

_____

Why do you think the cross and forgiveness has been emphasized so much more than the resurrection and the new life in Christ?

_____

_____

_____

_____

What effect has the "good news" of Christ had on you personally?

_____

_____

_____

How have you not fully embraced your new life in Christ and let go of the past?

_____

_____

_____

It is advantageous to each one for him to perceive his own particular nature and the grace of God. For he who does not perceive his own weakness and the divine favor . . . not having tested himself nor having condemned himself, will imagine that the benefit conferred upon him by the grace of heaven is his own doing. And this imagination also produces vanity, which will be the cause of his downfall. . . . They have been revealed to babes—to those who after childhood have come to better things. These are those who remember that it is not so much from their own effort as by the unspeakable goodness [of God] that they have reached the greatest possible extent of blessedness.

Origen (AD 184–253)

2

Forgiveness of Sins

Hebrews 9:11–28

Key Point

Christ is the only perfect sacrifice that atones for all of our past, present, and future sins.

Key Verse

How much more, then, will the blood of Christ, who through the eternal Spirit offered himself unblemished to God, cleanse our consciences from acts that lead to death.

Hebrews 9:14

History is God's story of redemption. God began to unfold His plan of redemption by establishing a covenant with Abraham. Abraham had been living in Haran when God forever changed his story by telling him to go to a land that He would reveal (see Genesis 12:1–3). God promised Abraham that his descendants would multiply and that from his seed would come the Messiah, who would be a blessing to all the peoples of the earth (see Matthew 1:1).

61

God continued His plan by forming a covenant with the nation of Israel through Moses (see Exodus 19–24). He gave them the Ten Commandments and set up a sacrificial system by which they could make atonement for their sins. However, as the writer of Hebrews would later state, this manmade sanctuary "was only a copy of the true one" that would come with the advent of Christ (Hebrews 9:24).

The sacrificial system set the stage for the coming of Jesus, who was the only perfect sacrifice who could atone for the sins of all people. "He did not enter by means of the blood of goats and calves; but he entered the Most Holy Place once for all by his own blood, thus obtaining eternal redemption" (Hebrews 9:12). Christ did not enter a "sanctuary made with human hands" but into "heaven itself . . . to appear for us in God's presence" (verse 24).

Under the Old Covenant, God's people had to present a sacrifice without spot or blemish as atonement for their sins (see Leviticus 4). This provided only a temporary covering of sin, for no animal could qualify as the perfect sacrifice needed to remove the stain of sin. Nor could any person qualify on the basis of his or her own righteousness, for all of humanity's "righteous acts are like filthy rags" (Isaiah 64:6). Only Jesus could serve as the perfect sacrifice. "God made him who had no sin to be sin for us, so that in him we might become the righteousness of God" (2 Corinthians 5:21).

Christ died "once for all" for our sins (Hebrews 9:12, 26), and no further sacrifice is needed. He forgave our past, present, and *future* sins—for when He died for all of our transgressions, all of our sins were in the future! This does not give us a license to keep on sinning but is just a gracious means by which we can approach God (see Romans 6:1–2). We confess our sins so we can walk in the light of Christ (see 1 John 1:5–9), but it is Jesus' death alone—not our confession—that makes forgiveness possible.

Jesus' perfect sacrifice provided the way for God to restore the relationship with humanity that had been lost during the Fall. Because of Jesus' willingness to bear all of our sins on the cross, that sin no longer separates us from God. The author of Hebrews concludes, "Therefore, brothers and sisters, since we have confidence to enter the Most Holy Place by the blood of Jesus . . . let us draw near to God with a sincere heart and with the full assurance that faith brings, having our hearts sprinkled to cleanse us" (Hebrews 10:19, 22).

Are your sins forgiven because you confessed them or because Christ died for them? Explain your answer.

_____

_____

_____

What was the purpose of the sacrificial system in the Old Testament? Why wasn't it enough to meet our needs today?

_____

_____

_____

There are no instructions in 1 John 1:5–9 admonishing Christians to ask God to forgive them, but we are instructed to confess our sins. What is the difference?

_____

_____

_____

How has knowing that you are forgiven for your past, present, and future sins affected the way you live?

_____

_____

_____

In Romans 6:1, Paul asks, "Shall we go on sinning so that grace may increase?" How would you answer this question?

_____

_____

_____

He is the God who is proclaimed in the Scriptures, to whom we were debtors, having transgressed His commandment. . . . Since He is the same One against whom we had sinned in the beginning. He is the One who grants forgiveness of sins in the end. . . . And in what way can sins be truly forgiven, unless it be that He against whom we have sinned has himself granted forgiveness "through the bowels of mercy of our God," in which "He has visited us" through His Son.

Irenaeus (AD 130–202)

3

New Life in Christ

John 6:25–59

Key Point

What Adam and Eve lost in the Fall was life, and what Jesus came to give us was life.

Key Verse

I am the living bread that came down from heaven. Whoever eats this bread will live forever. This bread is my flesh, which I will give for the life of the world.

John 6:51

In the gospel of John, we read the story of how Jesus fed more than 5,000 people with two small fish and five loaves of bread. The next day, after the miracle of walking on water, He arrived on the other shore of the Sea of Galilee. The people learned He was there and got into their boats to go in search of Him.

When they found Him, Jesus said, "You are looking for me, not because you saw the signs I performed but because you ate the loaves and had your fill" (John 6:26). He went on to remind the people that when the Israelites were in the wilderness, God sustained them by providing them with a daily portion of manna, or "bread from heaven" (Exodus 16:4). He then said, "I am the bread of life" (John 6:35).

Most of the people who heard this claim immediately protested, because they identified Jesus as only the son of Joseph (see verse 42), not even to be compared with Moses. Jesus countered by saying that Moses didn't give the Israelites the bread—it came from heaven. Furthermore, though the manna sustained the people's physical lives, it could not give them eternal/ spiritual life. Jesus, like the manna, had come from heaven, but unlike the manna—which could only satisfy the people's need temporarily—Jesus was offering the bread of eternal life. What Adam and Eve lost was life, and Jesus came to restore that life (see John 10:10).

Earlier in John's story of Jesus, a man named Nicodemus had asked Christ how to receive this bread of life. Nicodemus was a member of the Jewish ruling council, and Jesus knew full well what was in his heart. He said to him, "Truly I tell you, no one can see the kingdom of God unless they are born again" (John 3:3). He told Nicodemus that he had been born physically alive, but to have eternal/spiritual life, he needed to be "born of water and the Spirit" (verse 5). The only way for Nicodemus to receive eternal life was to believe in Jesus and trust in His works. As Paul would later write, "For it is by grace you have been saved, through faith—and this is not from yourselves, it is the gift of God—not by works, so that no one can boast" (Ephesians 2:8–9).

New life in Christ—eternal and spiritual life—is given to us the moment we are born again. If we do not receive this "second birth" before we physically die, all we have to look forward to is an eternity without Christ. Jesus is our life (see Colossians 3:4)—the way, the truth and the *life* (see John 14:6). If we have been born again, our names are written in the book of *life* (see Philippians 4:3).

To be *spiritually* alive means that our souls are in union with God. It means that we are alive "in Christ" and that Christ is in us. The "life of Christ" is much more than a historical account of the 33 years that He appeared in the flesh—it is what every born again believer *has within him or her*. It means that we are again united with God but also that we have the power of His presence to live a righteous life.

Read John 6:30–33. What did the people ask Jesus to provide so they could believe in Him? How did Jesus respond?

_____

_____

_____

What did Jesus mean when He told the people that He was the bread of life?

_____

_____

_____

What did Jesus tell Nicodemus that he must do to receive eternal/spiritual life? How do we receive that life?

_____

_____

_____

What are the practical ramifications of knowing that your soul is in union with God?

_____

_____

_____

What confidence can you draw from "Christ in you, the hope of glory" (Colossians 1:27)?

_____

_____

_____

In this manner, the Lord has redeemed us through His own blood, giving His soul for our souls, and His flesh for our flesh. He has also poured out the Spirit of the Father for the union and communion of God and man, actually imparting God to men by means of the Spirit. On the other hand, He has joined man to God by His own incarnation. And He will truly and lastingly bestow immortality upon us at His coming—through communion with God.

Irenaeus (AD 130–202)

4

New Identity in Christ

John 1:1–14

Key Point

The Father sent Jesus in order that we might become children of God.

Key Verse

Yet to all who did receive him, to those who believed in his name, he gave the right to become children of God.

John 1:12

I n God's unfolding story there was no new revelation from heaven for more than 400 years when suddenly, "The Word became flesh and made his dwelling among us. We have seen his glory, the glory of the one and only Son, who came from the Father, full of grace and truth" (John 1:14).

To the Greek philosophers, the "word" (*logos*) was the ultimate of intellectual pursuits; the rational principle that governs the universe. Now it is revealed that this highest of philosophical notion had become incarnate—that is, it took on a human form. Jesus not only spoke the truth;

He is the truth and in Him there is no darkness at all (see 1 John 1:5). "In him was life, and that life was the light of all mankind" (John 1:4). Notice that light does not produce life; rather, the eternal life of God is the light of the world.

The first Adam was born both physically and spiritually alive, but he sinned and died spiritually. This last Adam was born of a virgin and was also physically and spiritually alive. Unlike the first Adam, he never sinned, even though He was tempted in every way. By His life He accomplished two tasks.

First, He gave us an example to follow in His steps. He showed us how a spiritually alive person could live a righteous life on planet earth. What He modeled was total dependence on His heavenly Father. He said, "By myself I can do nothing" (John 5:30); "I live because of the Father" (6:57); "I have come here from God. I have not come on my own; God sent me" (8:42); "The words I say to you I do not speak on my own authority. Rather, it is the Father, living in me, who is doing his work" (14:10); "Now they know that everything you have given me comes from you" (17:7).

Second, Jesus came that we might have life, and receiving that life by faith brings us a new identity. "Yet to all who did receive him, to those who believed in his name, he gave the right to become children of God—children born not of natural descent, nor of human decision or a husband's will, but born of God" (John 1:12–13). "The Spirit himself testifies with our spirit that we are God's children" (Romans 8:16).

"How great is the love the Father has lavished on us, that we should be called children of God! And that is what we are! The reason the world does not know us is that it did not know him. Dear friends, now we are children of God, and what we will be has not yet been made known. But we know that when Christ appears, we shall be like him, for we shall see him as he is. All who have this hope in him purify themselves, just as he is pure" (1 John 3:2–3). Believers are not in the process of becoming children of God; they are children of God who are in the process of becoming like Christ. Who we are determines what we do, and God wants us to know that we are His children.

People cannot consistently behave in a way that is inconsistent with what they believe about themselves. Consequently, we will struggle with a negative self-perception to the degree that we don't see ourselves the way God sees us. Knowing who we really are in Christ meets our needs for acceptance, security, and significance (see In Christ chart on following page).

What was markedly different between the first Adam and the Last Adam?

Where do natural people derive their identity?

Why is knowing who we are "in Christ" so important?

What does it mean to you personally to know that you are a child of God? What difference does that make?

How has Christ met all of your needs for acceptance, security, and significance?

_____

_____

_____

By writing these things John is exhorting his readers to recognize what it means to be born again of God. He tells them that they are now worthy to be loved as children of God, even in this world, and that the adoption of sons is a reality here and now. For since we now know in part and have the first fruits of the Spirit, we already have something of the adoption of sons and can see what the fullness of it will be when it arrives.

Didymus the Blind (AD 313–398)

In Christ

I Am Accepted

John 1:12	I am God's child
John 15:15	I am Christ's friend
Romans 5:1	I have been justified
1 Corinthians 6:17	I am united with the Lord and one with Him in spirit
1 Corinthians 6:20	I have been bought with a price—I belong to God
1 Corinthians 12:27	I am a member of Christ's body
Ephesians 1:1	I am a saint
Ephesians 1:5	I have been adopted as God's child
Ephesians 2:18	I have direct access to God through the Holy Spirit
Colossians 1:14	I have been redeemed and forgiven of all my sins
Colossians 2:10	I am complete in Christ

I Am Secure

Romans 8:1–2	I am free from condemnation
Romans 8:28	I am assured that all things work together for good
Romans 8:31	I am free from any condemning charges against me
Romans 8:35	I cannot be separated from the love of God
2 Corinthians 1:21–22	I have been established, anointed, and sealed by God
Colossians 3:3	I am hidden with Christ in God
Philippians 1:6	I am confident that the good work that God has begun in me will be perfected
Philippians 3:20	I am a citizen of heaven
2 Timothy 1:7	I have not been given a spirit of fear, but of power, love, and a sound mind
Hebrews 4:16	I can find grace and mercy in time of need
1 John 5:18	I am born of God and the evil one cannot touch me

I Am Significant

Matthew 5:13–14	I am the salt and light of the earth
John 15:1, 5	I am a branch of the true vine, a channel of His life
John 15:16	I have been chosen and appointed to bear fruit
Acts 1:8	I am a personal witness of Christ
1 Corinthians 3:16	I am God's temple
2 Corinthians 5:17	I am a minister of reconciliation
2 Corinthians 6:1	I am God's co-worker
Ephesians 2:6	I am seated with Christ in the heavenly realm
Ephesians 2:10	I am God's workmanship
Ephesians 3:12	I may approach God with freedom and confidence
Philippians 4:13	I can do all things through Christ who strengthens me

5

The Defeat of Satan

1 John 3:7–15

Key Point

The kingdom of God triumphs over the kingdom of darkness.

Key Verse

The reason the Son of God appeared was to destroy the devil's work.

1 John 3:8

God's story for us, as revealed in the pages of the Bible, is that Christ died for our sins and gave us eternal life. This is certainly good news, but the story would not be complete if Jesus had not also defeated the devil at the cross. "The reason the Son of God appeared was to destroy the devil's work" (1 John 3:8).

John calls Satan the "evil one" (1 John 3:12) and credits him with being the instigator of human sin and depravity. He had been sinning "from the beginning" (verse 8), even before the fall of Adam and Eve, for he had rebelled against God. In the Garden of Eden, he tried to thwart God's plans by tempting Adam and Eve to sin. His plan was successful, but even in his triumph God promised that the Messiah would come through the seed of the woman to crush his head (see Genesis 3:14–15).

Satan worked to further disrupt God's plan by destroying the bloodline from which the Messiah would come. He influenced Cain, "who belonged to the evil one" (1 John 3:12), to kill Abel, but God gave Eve another child (see Genesis 4:25). His name was Seth, which means "restitution," and the Messiah descended from his line. Satan later tried to eliminate Moses and Jesus by having all the young boys in their vicinity killed (see Exodus 1:22; Matthew 2:16), but God provided a way for them to be spared.

Jesus triumphed over Satan and defeated him, but Peter warns us, "Be alert and of sober mind. Your enemy the devil prowls around like a roaring lion looking for someone to devour" (1 Peter 5:8). He is like a deadly bee, but those of us who belong to Christ know his stinger has been removed. We are children of God and cannot be touched by the evil one (see 1 John 4:1–4; 5:18–19). For our protection, John admonishes us to walk in the light (see 1 John 1:7), confess our sins (see 1 John 1:9), obey God's Word (see 1 John 2:5), and love one another (see 1 John 4:7).

John also warns us not to love the world or anything in it (see 1 John 2:15). The channels of temptation that Satan used to deceive Eve and cause Adam to sin are the same ones he used to tempt Jesus—and they are the same ones he is now using against all the children of God (see verse 16). We must be aware that there are many "antichrists" in the world today who belong to the evil one and strive to thwart God's plan and the work of Christ. For this reason, John tells us to "not believe every spirit, but test the spirits to see whether they are from God" (1 John 4:1).

The battle for the souls of humans will continue until the Lord returns, but we have the assurance of eternal life (see 5:13) and answered prayer (see verse 15). Furthermore, as John concludes, "We know also that the Son of God has come and has given us understanding, so that we may know him who is true. And we are in him who is true by being in his Son Jesus Christ. He is the true God and eternal life" (verse 20).

What attempts did Satan make—and is still making—to thwart God's plan?

_____

_____

_____

What are the three channels that Satan used to tempt Eve, Jesus, and God's children?

_____

_____

_____

What assurance does God give us that we can triumph over the devil's schemes?

_____

_____

_____

Given that Satan has been disarmed, in what ways are we still vulnerable?

_____

_____

_____

As a believer, how important is it that you know that the "bee" has no stinger?

_____

_____

_____

It was necessary that through man himself Satan would, when conquered, be bound with the same chains with which he had bound man. This was so that man, being set free, could return to his Lord, leaving to Satan those bonds by which himself had been fettered—that is, sin. For when Satan is bound, man is set free. Satan is justly led captive, for he had led men unjustly into bondage. At the same time, man, who had been led captive in times past, was rescued from the grasp of his possessor, according to the tender mercy of God the Father. For He had compassion on His own handiwork, and gave salvation to it.

Irenaeus (AD 130–202)

Reality Check

If you died tonight, do you know where you would spend eternity? Would you be with God in heaven? The apostle Paul admonishes everyone to "examine yourselves to see whether you are in the faith; test yourselves. Do you not realize that Christ Jesus is in you—unless you fail the test?" (2 Corinthians 13:5). Attending religious services won't save you. Trying to live a righteous life won't save you. Practicing spiritual disciplines won't save you. Participating in Christian ordinances won't save you. Only by the grace of God can you be saved, and there is only one definitive test: "He who has the Son has life; he who does not have the Son of God does not have life" (1 John 5:12).

Salvation is a gift from God. It is free because Jesus paid the price. He did for us what we could not do for ourselves. "For it is by grace you have been saved, through faith—and this not from yourselves, it is the gift of God—not by works, so that no one can boast" (Ephesians 2:8–9). Grace is God's unmerited favor to the spiritually dead and sinful inhabitants of this fallen world. You can't earn grace; you can only humbly receive it as a free gift.

We only have one hope in our sinful state, and that is to throw ourselves on the mercy of God. If by the grace of God we receive mercy in this lifetime, we shall not have to face what we justly deserve in eternity. If God gave us what we deserve, we would all reap eternal damnation. Those who cry out for mercy are acknowledging their guilt, asking not to be given what they justly deserve. The good news is, "He saved us, not because of righteous things we had done, but because of his mercy" (Titus 3:5). "Everyone who calls on the name of the Lord will be saved" (Romans 10:13). "Yet to all who did receive him, to those who believed in his name, he gave the right to become children of God" (John 1:12). You can receive Christ right now by choosing to believe that Jesus died for your sins on the cross and was resurrected in order that you may have eternal life. You can make your choice to trust only in Christ and receive Him into your life by verbally expressing the following:

Dear heavenly Father, I confess that I have sinned and that I am a sinner by nature. I know that I am spiritually dead because of my sin and not worthy to be Your child. I am in great need of Your grace and I throw myself on Your mercy. I am sorry for my sins and I humbly ask for Your forgiveness. I choose to believe that Jesus died for my sins on the cross, and I choose to believe that He came to give me eternal life. As an act of faith, I receive You into my life. I pray that You would enable me to be the person that You created me to be. I choose from this day forward to repent by turning away from sin to live a righteous life by faith in the power of the Holy Spirit. I ask all this in the wonderful name of Jesus, whom I confess to be my Lord and my Savior. Amen.

Did you call on the name of the Lord? Do you believe in your heart that Jesus died for your sins and that He was raised from the dead in order that you may have eternal life? Is Jesus the Lord of your life? If you can say yes to those questions, then you are a child of God and a member of the Body of Christ. Welcome to the family of God. There is nothing more that you could do to ensure your salvation, because you have not been saved by your good deeds. Salvation is a free gift from God, and you have just received it.

All God asks of you is to be the person He created you to be and to glorify Him by living a righteous life. Why don't you thank Him for sending Jesus to die in your place in order that you may be forgiven and have eternal life.

You may not be fully aware of everything that transpired the moment you made your decision for Christ. All the angels in heaven rejoiced when you made that profession of faith. God became your heavenly Father. Your body became a temple of God. The Holy Spirit will guide you into all truth. Start your spiritual journey by making your decision public by being baptized in a local church. Seek healthy relationships with other believers. Attend a Bible-believing church regularly and finish the VICTORY SERIES, which will ground you in your faith. And now, may:

> The LORD bless you and keep you;
> The LORD make his face shine on you
> And be gracious to you;
> The LORD turn his face toward you
> And give you peace.
>
> Numbers 6:24–26

The Story of God's Sanctification

Back to the saga of the Potter and the clay. Although the prince of darkness was defeated, the Potter allowed him and all his evil spirits to continue roaming across planet earth until final judgment came upon them. Their plan was to blind the minds of the unbelieving pots so they could never hear the good news that the Divine Pot had come to die for their sins and give them new life. Many believed this lie, never received their pardon, and remained dead with all their impurities. Others believed the truth and were instantly forgiven, and they received the eternal life offered by the Divine Pot. However, the evil one continued to tempt, accuse, and deceive the forgiven pots, enticing them to believe his lies.

To all the pots that heard the good news and responded to the truth, the Potter sent His Spirit to guide and bear witness that they truly were children of the Potter. He said to them, "Like clay in the hand of the potter, so are you in my hand" (Jeremiah 18:6). Because these redeemed pots had become misshaped by the world, He had to reform them into His likeness.

These new creations could not be remade on their own, but it was their responsibility to become more and more like the Potter. Although they would have many other useful purposes for remaining on planet earth, nothing was more important to the Potter than to have all His redeemed pots free from their awful past and become pure like Him.

Daily Readings

1. Sound Doctrine	2 Timothy 3:10–17
2. Justified by Faith	Romans 3:10–31
3. Becoming Like Jesus	1 Thessalonians 4:1–12
4. Positional Sanctification	2 Peter 1:3–11
5. Progressive Sanctification	1 Peter 1:3–16

1

Sound Doctrine

2 Timothy 3:10–17

Key Point

The Word of God instructs us, rebukes us, corrects us, and trains us on how to live righteously, and equips us for every good work.

Key Verse

Sanctify them by the truth; your word is truth.

John 17:17

Jesus had defeated the work of Satan. He had "disarmed the powers and authorities" and "made a public spectacle of them, triumphing over them by the cross" (Colossians 2:15). Christ's sacrifice for our sins signaled the end of the story for the devil. Yet we still live in a fallen world, and until Christ returns and casts Satan into the lake of fire (see Revelation 20:1–15), we will face many hardships as we live out our stories on earth.

Just before Jesus departed this world to be with the Father, He prayed for all the believers, saying, "My prayer is not that you take them out of the world but that you protect them from the evil one. They are not of the world, even as I am not of it. Sanctify them by the truth; your word is truth" (John 17:15–17). God's Word is a lamp for our feet and a light on our path (see Psalm 119:105). It is the only infallible truth that can set us free, serve as the basis for our sanctification, and protect us from deception.

The apostle Paul instructed Timothy, "All Scripture is God-breathed and is useful for teaching, rebuking, correcting and training in righteousness, so that the servant of God may be thoroughly equipped for every good work" (2 Timothy 3:16–17). In this passage, Paul explains the purpose for God's Word. First, the written Word is "God-breathed," or inspired, by the Lord. The Holy Spirit guided the men who wrote it so that their writings were without error (see 2 Peter 1:20–21).

God's Word is also profitable for teaching. In making this statement, Paul was saying that the Bible is a source of authority for teaching—that it contains *sound doctrine*. The Word of God provides guidance for ethical instruction (see 1 Timothy 1:9–20) and enables believers to mature in Christ. A follower of Christ "must hold firmly to the trustworthy message as it has been taught, so that he can encourage others by sound doctrine and refute those who oppose it" (Titus 1:9).

When correctly taught and applied, the Word of God will rebuke, correct, train us to live righteously, and thoroughly equip us for every good work. Sin will keep us from God's Word, but God's Word will keep us from sinning. His Word will rebuke us when we are wrong and correct us so we don't do it again—all with the purpose of enabling us to live righteously. God never intended His Word to be discussed on a purely intellectual level and not put into practice. Rather, "the word of God is alive and active . . . it judges the thoughts and attitudes of the heart" (Hebrews 4:12).

The danger is thinking the Word of God is profitable for teaching and training in competence, instead of training in righteousness. That bypasses the reproof and correction that is necessary for repentance. Information without transformation is malformation. People may become more knowledgeable when that happens, but not necessarily more mature. Scripture emphasizes being before doing, character before career, and maturity before ministry. We can't be the people God created us to be unless His Word penetrates our hearts and transforms our lives. When that happens we become

"God's handiwork, created in Christ Jesus to do good works, which God prepared in advance for us to do" (Ephesians 2:10).

Review 2 Timothy 3:10–17. What kinds of trials did Paul face while serving the Lord? What promise does Paul make to Timothy about trials?

_____

_____

_____

_____

How can we be kept from the evil one?

_____

_____

_____

In what ways will the Bible equip you to do the work of God?

_____

_____

_____

How can you get beyond an intellectual knowledge of the Bible to total transformation?

_____

_____

_____

_____

In regard to the Church, the first concern of our Lord is that we be kept from evil. How well do you think you and others are equipped to stand against the evil forces?

_____

_____

_____

The divinity of Scripture—which extends to all of it—is not [lost] because of the inability of our weakness to discover in every expression the hidden splendor of the doctrines veiled in common and unattractive phraseology. For we have the "treasure in earthen vessels" so that the Excellency of the power of God may shine forth. For if the usual methods of demonstration used by men . . . had been successful in convincing us, then our faith would rightly have been thought to rest on the wisdom of men—not on the power of God. However, now it is evident to everyone who lifts up his eyes that the word and preaching have not prevailed among the multitude "by persuasive words of wisdom, but by the demonstration of the Spirit and of power."

Origen (AD 184–253)

2

Justified by Faith

Romans 3:10–31

Key Point

Believers are justified before God and forgiven the moment they put their faith in Him.

Key Verses

Therefore, since we have been justified through faith, we have peace with God through our Lord Jesus Christ, through whom we have gained access by faith into this grace in which we now stand.

Romans 5:1–2

The apostle Paul addresses the crucial question as to how we can be justified before a perfect and holy God, since "there is no one righteous, not even one" (Romans 3:10). For God must hold us accountable for our actions according to His law, and without justification we can never be acquitted for our sins. "No one will be declared righteous in God's sight by the works of the law; rather, through the law we become conscious of our sin" (verse 20).

The Word of God declares that we have missed the mark of God's standard for holiness. We are all sinful by nature and can never do enough good works to gain acquittal. We cannot render judgment on ourselves because we are always guilty, and a just God cannot render us just by our works. This is the dilemma of all humanity! The atonement of Christ is the answer. In Him alone we receive justification.

The word "justification" means "to make righteous" or "to do righteousness." It is the righteousness of God that justifies us, not our own "personal" righteousness. As Paul states, "Righteousness is given through faith in Jesus Christ to all who believe. . . . A person is justified by faith apart from observing the law" (verses 22, 28). This does not mean that God overlooks our sin or fails to judge us as sinners, for doing so would deny the integrity of God and destroy the concept of justification. God's justice and holiness *demands* payment for sin, and Jesus paid that penalty at the cross. By allowing Christ to die in our place for our transgressions, God maintained His justice and enabled us to be saved from our sins (see verse 26).

In the Old Testament, the people made blood sacrifices to God to atone for or wipe away their sins. In this way, it was possible for them to temporarily reconcile with God. When Jesus came to earth, He offered His life as a blood sacrifice once and for all to cover, or take away, the sins of all humankind. As Paul wrote, "The death he died, he died to sin once for all" (Romans 6:10).

Note that justification does not mean universal salvation, but rather universal grace and forgiveness. God pronounced that all can be forgiven in Christ, but not everyone will receive this gift of salvation (see Romans 10:14–17). There are only two unforgiveable sins. The first is the denial of sin, because, by its nature, there is nothing to forgive. The second is the denial of Christ. Jesus said, "Unless you believe that I AM who I claim to be, you will die in your sins" (John 8:24 NLT).

God justifies and forgives all people the moment they put their faith in Him. "Therefore, since we have been justified through faith, we have peace with God through our Lord Jesus Christ, through whom we have gained access by faith into this grace in which we now stand" (Romans 5:1–2). Our faith in Jesus joins us together with God, and He clothes us in His righteousness. When that occurs, "there is now no condemnation for those who are in Christ Jesus" (Romans 8:1).

Read Romans 3:19–26. What does God's law reveal to us?

_____

_____

_____

Why couldn't God just choose to forgive us, and the matter would be settled?

_____

_____

_____

Why could the sacrifice of Jesus atone for our sin, but no effort on our part could?

_____

_____

_____

How would your life (and the lives of others) be impacted if you knew for certain that you were totally justified before God and all your sins were forgiven?

_____

_____

_____

You may never have access to the leadership of countries and companies, but you have access to Almighty God. What does that incredible privilege mean to you?

_____

_____

_____

Paul has discussed the point that nobody is justified by works, but all are justified by faith, and he has proved this by the example of Abraham, of whom the Jews claim to be the only children. He has also explained why neither race nor circumcision makes people children of Abraham, but only faith, because Abraham was initially justified by faith alone. Now, having concluded this argument, Paul urges both Jews and Gentiles to live at peace, because no one is saved by his own merit, but everyone is saved in the same way, by God's grace. "Peace with God" means either that both sides should submit to God or that we should have the peace of God and not just the peace of the world.

Pelagius (AD 390–418)

3

Becoming Like Jesus
1 Thessalonians 4:1–12

Key Point

God sanctifies us and removes the pollution of sin from our lives the moment we put our faith in Him.

Key Verse

It is God's will that you should be sanctified.

1 Thessalonians 4:3

God's story for us began when He said, "Let us make mankind in our image, in our likeness" (Genesis 1:26). Fallen humanity still has remnants of being created in God's image. That is what separates them from the rest of creation. Animals operate out of divine instinct, but humans have the capacity to think, feel, and choose. What we have all lost is the likeness in character and righteousness, for we have all sinned and fallen short of the glory of God.

In 1 Thessalonians 4:3, Paul writes, "It is God's will that you should be sanctified." Sanctification is the process of becoming more and more like Jesus. It is the gracious work of the Lord by which He progressively delivers us—justified believers—from the pollution of sin, transforms our character to be like His own, and enables us to bear fruit for His kingdom. When God sanctifies us, He sets us apart from sin and sinful behavior so we can be righteous and live a righteous life.

Justification is the act of a judge, while sanctification is the act of a priest. Through justification, God declares us righteous because of the righteousness of Christ, which is accounted to us. Through sanctification, God removes the pollution of sin from our lives. The process of justification is completed when we experience new birth in Christ and accept His sacrifice for our sins. For believers, it is always referred to in the past tense. Sanctification, however, begins at our new birth and is completed in heaven.

The Bible reveals that sanctification, like salvation, occurs in the past, present, and future. We have been saved (see Ephesians 2:4–5, 8), we are being saved (see 1 Corinthians 1:18), and we shall someday be fully saved from the wrath that is to come (see Romans 5:9–10). Even though we haven't yet experienced all that salvation brings, God wants us to have the assurance of salvation (see 1 John 5:13), and the presence of the Holy Spirit in our lives is our guarantee (see Ephesians 1:14). In the same way, we have been sanctified (see Acts 20:32), we are being sanctified (see Romans 6:22), and we shall someday be fully sanctified in heaven (see 1 Thessalonians 5:23–24).

When sanctification is referred to in the past tense, it is commonly called "positional sanctification." When sanctification is referred to in the present tense it is commonly called "progressive sanctification." Both are important in understanding the process by which we become like Jesus. Our sanctification began when we received Christ as our Savior, but if we viewed it as a completed action, it might lead us to believe we are perfectly righteous when we are not.

Positional sanctification is the basis for progressive sanctification. Christians are not trying to become children of God—they *are* children of God who are becoming like Christ. It is through progressive sanctification that we work out our salvation (see Philippians 2:12) and make real our experience of the new life in Christ. We live "in order to please God" (1 Thessalonians 4:1), knowing that "God did not call us to be impure, but to live a holy life" (verse 7). For this reason, "Anyone who rejects this instruction does not reject a human being but God, the very God who gives you his Holy Spirit" (verse 8).

What is the difference between being created in God's image and being created in God's likeness?

_____

_____

_____

How is sanctification different from justification?

_____

_____

_____

What are the dangers of focusing only on positional sanctification (it's a done deal) or seeing only progressive sanctification (trying to become somebody you already are)?

_____

_____

_____

Have you been fully saved? Fully sanctified? Partially saved? Partially sanctified? Explain.

_____

_____

_____

How are you "working out" your salvation? What changes can you see now in your life that show you are becoming more like Jesus every day?

Christ was made like a lamb who is dumb before her shearer, so that we might be purified by His death. For His death is given as a sort of medicine against the opposing power and also against the sin of those who open their minds to the truth. For the death of Christ reduced to weakness those powers that war against the human race. And it set the life of each believer free from sin through a power beyond our words. He takes away sin until every enemy will be destroyed and death last of all—in order that the whole world may be free from sin. Therefore, John pointed to Him and said, "Behold! The Lamb of God who takes away the sin of the world."

Origen (AD 184–253)

4

Positional Sanctification

2 Peter 1:3–11

Key Point

The beauty of holiness transforms our lives and the world around us.

Key Verse

We have been made holy through the sacrifice of the body of Jesus Christ once for all.

Hebrews 10:10

Each of us who has accepted Jesus as our Lord and Savior has a "testimony" or story to share about how we came to make that decision. For many of us, choosing to follow Christ brought us out of darkness and led us to making profound and positive changes. A few had parents who modeled the benefits of a life devoted to following God, and we naturally wanted to experience those same benefits in our lives. Regardless of our particular story, the reality is that we were *all* sinners before we met God.

We all needed to receive justification for our sins and be set on the path of sanctification.

When Paul shared the story of his salvation with King Agrippa in Acts 26, he explained how God had commissioned him to open the eyes of the Gentiles and "turn them from darkness to light, and from the power of Satan to God, so that they may receive forgiveness of sins and a place among those who are sanctified by faith" (verse 18). Paul's mission was to bring the gospel to the lost so they could be forgiven, rescued from the dominion of darkness, and brought into the kingdom of God (see Colossians 1:13). Safely in the hands of their heavenly Father, sinners became saints, failures became victories, and the common was made holy.

One of the cities to which Paul had been sent was Corinth. Paul opened his first letter to this body of believers with this greeting: "To the church of God in Corinth, to those sanctified in Christ Jesus and called to be his holy people" (1 Corinthians 1:2). Later in the letter, he asked the congregation to recall their former way of life and said, "But you were washed, you were sanctified, you were justified in the name of the Lord Jesus Christ and by the Spirit of our God" (1 Corinthians 6:11). Paul wanted to remind the believers of their *positional* sanctification, which took place at their salvation.

Just as the "past tense" reality of our salvation is the basis for the "present tense" working out of our salvation, so also is our position in Christ the basis for our growth in Christ. At the moment of our salvation, we are set apart, or separated, to God and begin to participate in His holiness. Peter states, "[God's] divine power has [past tense] given us everything we need for a godly life through our knowledge of him who called us by his own glory and goodness. Through these he has given [past tense] us his very great and precious promises, so that through them you may participate in the divine nature and escape the corruption in the world caused by evil desires" (2 Peter 1:3–4).

Positional holiness is based on the fact that we are new creations in Christ (see 2 Corinthians 5:17). By faith we are joined to Christ and share in His holiness. This does not mean we are sinless and perfect—just that we are spiritually alive in Christ. As sinners we couldn't enter into God's presence, but through our faith in Christ—who sacrificed Himself to cleanse us from sin—we are joined to Him and have been invited into the "holy of holies" of heaven to have fellowship with Him. It is from this lofty position in Christ that we grow in grace.

Read 2 Peter 1:3–11. What are we given the moment we are born again?

_____

_____

_____

What characteristics will define our lives and reveal that we have been sanctified or "set apart" for God?

_____

_____

_____

What hope does it provide for us knowing that our union with God makes us a participant in the divine nature?

_____

_____

_____

What is preventing you and others from being holy as Christ is holy? (For instance, "I don't want to give up certain pleasures," "I would feel like a nerd," "I tried once and it didn't work," "I fear rejection," "I don't know how," "I will later," "I just don't care.")

_____

_____

_____

What would you stand to gain if you became more like Jesus?

Whom He has made rich, none will make poor. For, in fact, there can be no poverty to him whose breast has once been supplied with heavenly food. Ceilings enriched in gold, and houses adorned with mosaics of costly marble, will seem crude to you now that you know that it is you yourself who are to be perfected, instead. . . . Let us embellish this "house" with the colors of innocence; let us enlighten it with the light of justice.

Cyprian (AD 200–258)

5

Progressive Sanctification

1 Peter 1:3–16

Key Point

God's will for our lives is our sanctification.

Key Verse

But now that you have been set free from sin and have become slaves to God, the benefit you reap leads to holiness, and the result is eternal life.

Romans 6:22

God's story has no beginning or end, but our story begins at the moment He calls us out of darkness to walk in His marvelous light. That is a beginning and not an end. It is God's will that we learn how to be holy as He is holy and take steps to make that a reality in our lives. The process of growing from spiritual babes to Christlikeness is commonly called "progressive sanctification." The Westminster Catechism defines this as, "The work of God's free grace, whereby we are renewed in the whole man after the image of God and are enabled more and more to die unto sin and live unto righteousness."

Paul describes this ongoing work in Colossians 2:6–7 when he writes, "Just as you received Christ Jesus as Lord, continue to live your lives in him, rooted and built up in him, strengthened in the faith as you were taught, and overflowing with thankfulness." Paul states that our first step in conforming to God's image is to be rooted in Christ, which refers to our positional sanctification. Once we are rooted in Christ, we can be built up in Him, which refers to progressive sanctification. Notice that the whole sanctification process is based on our union with God, which is what it means to be "in Christ." If there is no spiritual life, we cannot grow spiritually.

God the Father is the primary agent of our sanctification "through the sanctifying work of the Spirit" (1 Peter 1:2). Additionally, we are also agents of our own sanctification. Peter states, "Prepare your minds for action, keep sober in spirit, fix your hope completely on the grace to be brought to you at the revelation of Jesus Christ. As obedient children, do not be conformed to the former lusts which were yours in your ignorance" (1 Peter 1:13–14 NASB). We have an active role in our own sanctification and must assume our responsibility for being all God created us to be.

However, as believers we must not be deceived into thinking that our sanctification comes about as a result of our own efforts. Paul admonished the Galatian believers on this point when he wrote, "Did you receive the Spirit by the works of the law, or by believing what you heard? Are you so foolish? After beginning by means of the Spirit, are you now trying to finish by means of the flesh?" (Galatians 3:2–3). We are saved by faith and sanctified by faith in God through the power of the Holy Spirit. That is why Jesus prayed, "Sanctify them by the truth; your word is truth" (John 17:17). We are not saved by how we behave, and neither are we sanctified that way. Behavior is just a product of what we choose to believe, which is why James wrote, "I will show you my faith by my deeds" (2:18).

The authors of the Bible present progressive sanctification as a challenge to believers. The world, the flesh, and the devil oppose the will of God, and therefore they are enemies of our sanctification. Therefore we are to "purify ourselves from everything that contaminates body and spirit, perfecting holiness out of reverence for God" (2 Corinthians 7:1) and to "make every effort to live in peace with everyone and to be holy; without holiness no one will see the Lord" (Hebrews 12:14).

Review 1 Peter 1:3–16. How does Peter remind his readers of the sanctification they received at the time of their salvation?

What part do trials and tribulations play in progressive sanctification?

How are we agents of our own sanctification while at the same time totally dependent on God to make that happen?

How could you become more balanced by being more concerned about who you are as a person in terms of godly character as opposed to what you do?

How could you become more balanced in your dependency on God and assuming your responsibility to become like Him?

_____

_____

_____

You are still in the world. You are still in the battlefield. You daily fight for your lives. So you must be careful, that . . . what you have begun to be with such a blessed commencement will be consummated in you. It is a small thing to have first received something. It is a greater thing to be able to keep what you have attained. Faith itself and the saving birth do not make you alive by merely being received. Rather, they must be preserved. It is not the actual attainment, but the perfecting, that keeps a man for God. The Lord taught this in His instruction when He said, "Look! You have been made whole. Sin no more, lest a worse thing come upon you." Solomon, Saul, and many others were able to keep the grace given to them so long as they walked in the Lord's ways. However, when the discipline of the Lord was forsaken by them, grace also forsook them.

Cyprian (AD 200–258)

The Story of God's Transforming Power

The Potter forgave the little clay pots and gave them new life, but they were used to running their own lives. Their distorted character was part of their natural existence, and it had affected the way they lived with one another. When confronted by other clay pots about their impurities, they learned to be defensive. Some would lie or blame other pots. All the natural pots struggled to get along. They would form in little groups and shun those who had different shades of grey, lower social status, or any other imperfections. They covered their insecurities with a pretense of power, but inwardly they knew it was only a delusion. Some struggled gallantly against the inevitable, but in the end there was only death.

New life had come, but all their finite minds had been programmed to live independently of the Potter. How should they now live? They had conformed to this world, but with their new life came a better way to live. Being their own god led to futility, but how should they relate to the Potter? Could they really trust Him and be honest with Him? Some of the restored pots kind of liked being their own god and not answering to anyone. So they continued to live as they always had. Others had trouble believing that they were indeed new creations, because they still looked the same and had a lot of the same old problems. Still others realized that if they continued to believe and think as they always had, life wouldn't appear very different. They correctly reasoned that they had to be honest with the Potter and learn from Him how to live as a liberated pot. Those who did were transformed by the renewing of their minds.

Daily Readings

1. The Cleansing of Confession	1 John 1:1–11
2. The Renewing of Repentance	2 Chronicles 7:11–22
3. The Message of Reconciliation	Psalm 32:1–11
4. The Goal of Instruction	1 Timothy 1:1–11
5. Growing in Grace	Colossians 1:9–14

1

The Cleansing of Confession
1 John 1:1–10

Key Point

Confession is living in conscious moral agreement with God.

Key Verse

If we confess our sins, he is faithful and just and will forgive us our sins and purify us from all unrighteousness.

1 John 1:9

Acknowledging or confessing our sin is the first step in any recovery program, and for many, it is the hardest step to take. Those who can't say, "I did it," will never be fully restored. Those who can are walking in the light.

When the authors of the New Testament use the word "confess," it literally means "to speak the same thing" or "to agree with." It is the opposite of denial, whether spoken or unspoken. Sometimes this refers to a public confession of faith, such as when Jesus said in Matthew 10:32,

"Whoever [confesses] me before others, I will also [confess] before my Father in heaven." Sometimes this refers to an act of praise, such as when Paul says, "Therefore I will [confess] you among the Gentiles; I will sing the praises of your name" (Romans 15:9). It can also mean the acknowledgment of sin (see 1 John 1:9).

When John wrote his first letter to the churches, his concern was that the believers had fellowship with God and with one another (see 1 John 1:2–4). He knew it would be impossible for them to have this type of fellowship if they were living in denial and covering up their sin. For this reason, he urged them to "walk in the light" (verse 7) as God is light and live in moral agreement with Him. Claiming "to be without sin" (verse 8) is self-deception and pollutes our relationships with God and one another, while confession leads to purification from unrighteousness.

Unconfessed sin hinders the relationship we have with God and others. However, as we walk in the light and speak the truth in love, God has made provision to cleanse us from whatever transgression would otherwise mar our fellowship with Him and others. Note that God does not forgive our sins because we confess them. Rather, He forgives us because "the blood of Jesus, his Son, purifies us from all sin" (1 John 1:7). The cross is the only moral ground on which God can forgive. Thus, failing to confess all our sins will not lead to eternal damnation. God is faithful to forgive us because He has *promised* to do so, and He is just because His Son died for our sins (see verse 9). Believers' destinies are not at stake if they fail to confess every sin, but their daily victory may be. Knowing that we are already forgiven is what enables us to live in conscious moral agreement with God. Besides, God already knows our moral condition.

John concludes by stating that if "we claim we have not sinned, we make him out to be a liar and his word is not in us" (verse 10). It is likely that those who claim to have never sinned haven't come to Christ in the first place, because they don't see the need of salvation. However, as far as we are concerned, John wants us to live a confessional life in which God not only removes the guilt of our sin (forgives us) but also the stain of our sin (cleanses us).

Confession brings healing to the soul. James writes, "Confess your sins to each other and pray for each other so that you may be healed" (James

5:16). Confession reunites people, leads to a breakthrough in community, and enables them to have fellowship with God and one another.

Review 1 John 1:1–10. What does John say he is proclaiming to the believers? What is the purpose for writing the letter to them?

_____

_____

_____

_____

Why is it impossible for a believer to claim to have fellowship with God and yet not walk in the light?

_____

_____

_____

Why is it harder to say "I did it" than "I'm sorry"?

_____

_____

_____

Why does God want you to confess your sins if you have already been forgiven?

_____

_____

_____

What is keeping you from living in conscious moral agreement with God and others?

_____

_____

_____

By the confession of all past sins, they may express the meaning even of the baptism of John. For the Scripture says: "They were baptized, confessing their own sins." To us, it is a matter for thankfulness if we now do publicly confess our iniquities or our depravities. For, by mortification of our flesh and spirit, we make satisfaction for our former sins. At the same time, we lay in advance the foundation of defenses against the temptations that will closely follow.

Tertullian (AD 160–220)

2

The Renewing of Repentance

2 Chronicles 7:11–22

Key Point

Walking in God's ways requires not only confession but also repentance and a turning from our old sinful ways.

Key Verse

If my people, who are called by my name, will humble themselves and pray and seek my face and turn from their wicked ways, then will I hear from heaven, and I will forgive their sin and will heal their land.

2 Chronicles 7:14

Confession is the first step in God's recovery program, but it is only a first step. We can't just admit we are wrong and not take the necessary steps to correct what we believe and how we live. Those who don't repent are caught up in the sin-confess-sin-confess-and-sin-again cycle. They will never get out of that cycle if that is all they are doing. We should sin, confess, and repent. Jesus said, "Repent and believe the good news!" (Mark 1:15).

John the Baptist prepared the way for the coming of Christ by telling people to "repent, for the kingdom of heaven has come near" (Matthew 3:2). He baptized those who responded to his message, but to the morally self-righteous he said, "You brood of vipers! Who warned you to flee from the coming wrath? Produce fruit in keeping with repentance" (verses 7–8). John insisted that a person's repentance be accompanied by the fruit of that repentance: a changed life.

The word "repentance" literally means "a change of mind resulting in a change of living." As we go through life, we all hold certain attitudes and beliefs toward God and ourselves and live accordingly. If one day we are enlightened by the truth or come under the conviction of sin, we may choose to confess our sins and decide to change. If we truly repent, we experience a change of mind and attitude and no longer live the way we did before. Others could witness the fruit of our repentance. However, if we do not change the way we live, we have not really repented of our sin.

Paul reaffirmed the necessity of repentance when he said to the Ephesian elders, "I have declared to both Jews and Greeks that they must turn to God in repentance and have faith in our Lord Jesus" (Acts 20:21). Later, he told King Agrippa, "I preached that they should repent and turn to God and demonstrate their repentance by their deeds" (Acts 26:20). In the Early Church, the members would literally face the west and say, "I renounce you, Satan, and all your works and all your ways." Then they would face the east and make a public profession of their faith. They renounced their sin and false beliefs and expressed their new faith in God.

Genuine repentance is not just a matter of professing a decision to change or save ourselves from the judgment of God. Such was the attitude of some believers in the Early Church, who would say they had repented, but then continued to do the same things for which they had judged others. Paul said to them, "Do you think you will escape God's judgment? Or do you show contempt for the riches of his kindness, forbearance and patience, not realizing that God's kindness is intended to lead you to repentance?" (Romans 2:3–4). God is the One who grants us repentance and enables us to escape the snares of the devil (see 2 Timothy 2:25–26).

God desires that all men and women be saved (see 2 Peter 3:9). The Lord said to the prophet Ezekiel, "I take no pleasure in the death of anyone, declares the Sovereign LORD. Repent and live!" (Ezekiel 18:32).

Review 2 Chronicles 7:11–16. What three things does God require the people to do to receive forgiveness and healing?

Why is confession alone not enough?

What did John the Baptist mean in Matthew 3:8 when he told the Pharisees and Sadducees to "produce fruit in keeping with repentance"?

Why have you not truly repented if you say that you have repented, but continue to live as you always have?

How can you personally stop the sin-confess-and-sin-again cycle?

_____

_____

_____

God welcomes the repentance of the sinner, for He loves the repentance that follows sins. For this Word of whom we speak alone is sinless. For to sin is natural and common to all. But to return [to God] after sinning is characteristic not of any man, but only of a man of worth.

Clement of Alexandria (AD 150–215)

3

The Message of Reconciliation

Psalm 32:1–11

Key point

God has commissioned the Church to proclaim the message and carry on the ministry of reconciliation.

Key Verses

For God was pleased to have all his fullness dwell in him, and through him to reconcile to himself all things, whether things on earth or things in heaven, by making peace through his blood, shed on the cross.

Colossians 1:19–20

The truth that God has made it possible for us to confess and repent of our sins so we can be *reconciled* with Him is the ultimate love story. Confession cleanses us from all unrighteousness, and repentance removes the barriers to our intimacy with God. All this results in reconciliation with God and others. The Church has been handed the message and ministry of reconciliation.

In Psalm 32:2, David writes, "Blessed is the one whose sin the LORD does not count against them and in whose spirit is no deceit." David was no stranger to transgressions. He had committed adultery with a woman named Bathsheba, and when his sin brought about an unwanted pregnancy, he arranged the death of her husband in an attempt to cover up what he had done. The Lord gave David plenty of time to repent of his sins, but when he didn't, He sent the prophet Nathan to confront him (see 2 Samuel 11–12). The guilt tore up David and made him physically sick (see Psalm 32:3–4). He finally confessed his transgressions to the Lord and received forgiveness (see verse 5).

In Romans 5:8, Paul writes, "But God demonstrates his own love for us in this: While we were still sinners, Christ died for us." God proved His love for us by initiating the process of reconciliation toward us *while we were sinners.* Paul continues, "Since we have now been justified by his blood, *how much more* shall we be saved from God's wrath through him!" (verse 9, emphasis added). God loved us enough to *sacrifice His only Son* for our sins so we could be saved from His wrath.

However, it is not enough for us to know that we have been saved from hell if we are still spiritually dead. Salvation brings us much more than the forgiveness of sins—it also brings us spiritual life in Christ. As Paul writes, "For if, while we were God's enemies, we were reconciled to him through the death of his Son, *how much more*, having been reconciled, shall we be saved through his life!" (verse 10, emphasis added). We have been offered forgiveness, new life in Christ, and also reconciliation with God. We are no longer alienated from Him. As Paul said to the Ephesian believers, "In him and through faith in him we may approach God with freedom and confidence" (Ephesians 3:12).

We may never get to be in the presence of today's leaders or celebrities or have an audience with them, but as children of God we have access to our heavenly Father 24 hours of every day. Criminals can have their sentences reduced and their lives spared, but "good" people wouldn't want to associate with them. God does!

Paul concludes, "All this is from God, who reconciled us to himself through Christ and gave us the ministry of reconciliation: that God was reconciling the world to himself in Christ, not counting people's sins against them. And he has committed to us the message of reconciliation. We are therefore Christ's ambassadors, as though God were making his appeal through us. We implore you on Christ's behalf: Be reconciled to God" (2 Corinthians 5:18–20). What amazing love!

In Psalm 32:1–2, what blessings does David say a person will receive who repents of his or her sins to God and receives forgiveness?

_____

_____

_____

What harmful effects did David suffer by not repenting of his sins and attempting to hide them from God?

_____

_____

_____

What advice does David provide in Psalm 32:8–10 for those who would likewise attempt to conceal their sin from God?

_____

_____

_____

Why is it necessary for all parties to confess and repent in order to be reconciled?

_____

_____

_____

How can or have you carried out the ministry of reconciliation?

_____

_____

_____

Can you see how great God's love is for us? Who was the offended party? He was. Who took the first steps toward reconciliation? He did. Some will say that He sent the Son in His place, but this is a misunderstanding. Christ did not come apart from the Father who sent Him. They were both involved together in the work of reconciliation.

John Chrysostom (AD 347–407)

4

The Goal of Instruction

1 Timothy 1:1–11

Key Point

Knowledge makes arrogance, but love edifies.

Key Verse

The goal of this command is love, which comes from a pure heart and a good conscience and a sincere faith.

1 Timothy 1:5

When Paul penned the words of 1 Timothy, he was concerned that believers were falling away in their walk with God and wanted to provide instruction to help get them back on track. So he urged Timothy to warn believers about listening to teachers of false doctrines (see verses 3–4); about falling back under the law, which was made for the unrighteous (see verses 8–11); about moving away from the faith and paying attention to deceiving spirits (see 4:1); and about the deceitfulness of riches (see 6:6–18). He exhorted Timothy to maintain sound doctrine, stay under authority and develop godly character. Above all, he said, "The goal of this command is love, which comes from a pure heart and a good conscience and a sincere faith" (1:5). You will know true disciples by their love (see John 13:35).

The greatest commandment is to "love the Lord your God with all your heart and with all your soul and with all your mind. . . . The second is like it: 'Love your neighbor as yourself'" (Matthew 22:37, 39). In other words, the whole purpose of God's Word is to help us love God and others. Paul wrote, "If I speak in the tongues of men or of angels, but do not have love, I am only a resounding gong or a clanging cymbal. If I have the gift of prophecy and can fathom all mysteries and all knowledge, and if I have a faith that can move mountains, but do not have love, I am nothing" (1 Corinthians 13:1–2). Paul also warned us that "knowledge puffs up while love builds up" (8:1). We can know theology and be arrogant, but we can't know God and be arrogant.

This is the goal of biblical instruction—to enable ourselves and others to progressively take on the character of God. God loves us, because "God is love" (1 John 4:16). It is His nature to love us, and we are partakers of that divine nature (see 2 Peter 1:4). The love of God is not dependent on the object, which is why God's love for us is unconditional. Jesus said, "If you love those who love you, what credit is that to you? Even sinners love those who love them" (Luke 6:32). This is what differentiates God's love (*agape*), from the brotherly love of humanity (*phileo*).

Love can be a noun (*agape*) or a verb (*agapeo*). It is referring to the character of God when used as a noun (God is love; love is patient). When used as a verb, love seeks to meet the needs of others. "For God so loved the world that he *gave* his one and only Son, that whoever believes in him shall not perish but have eternal life" (John 3:16). The corollary of that verse for believers is 1 John 3:16–18: "This is how we know what love is: Jesus Christ laid down his life for us. And we ought to lay down our lives for our brothers and sisters. If anyone has material possessions and sees a brother or sister in need but has no pity on him, how can the love of God be in that person? Dear children, let us not love with words or tongue, but with actions and in truth." When we take on the character of God, we will be moved to meet the needs of others even when they are not very loveable.

Read 1 Timothy 1:3–7. What were some of the issues that the believers were facing?

_____

_____

_____

_____

What is the main difference between God's love and brotherly love?

_____

_____

_____

What does it say about us if we love only those who love us?

_____

_____

_____

_____

What will eventually happen if you make a personal goal of obtaining knowledge instead of becoming more loving?

_____

_____

_____

_____

Saying you don't love someone is an indictment of whom? Why?

_____

_____

_____

Loving one's enemies does not mean loving wickedness, ungodliness, adultery, or theft. Rather, it means loving the thief, the ungodly person, and the adulterer. Not as far as he sins (in respect of the actions by which he stains the name of man), but as he is a man and is the work of God.

Clement of Alexandria (AD 150–215)

5

Growing in Grace

Colossians 1:9–14

Key Point

True followers of Jesus are known by their fruit.

Key Verses

We continually ask God to fill you with the knowledge of his will through all the wisdom and understanding that the Spirit gives, so that you may live a life worthy of the Lord and please him in every way: bearing fruit in every good work, growing in the knowledge of God.

Colossians 1:9–10

Jesus said, "I am the vine; you are the branches. If you remain in me and I in you, you will bear much fruit" (John 15:5). True followers of Jesus will be known for their fruit (Matthew 7:20). Bearing fruit is the evidence that we are growing in the grace and knowledge of our Lord Jesus Christ. This process of growth is like a circular spiral that is ever-reaching toward heaven. In Colossians 1:9–12, Paul explains how this cycle of growth functions in our lives.

Cycle of Growth

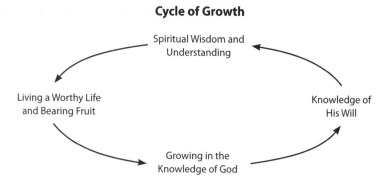

Spiritual Wisdom and
Understanding

Living a Worthy Life
and Bearing Fruit

Knowledge of
His Will

Growing in the
Knowledge of God

The cycle of growth begins with the knowledge of God's Word. The truth then enters our hearts resulting in wisdom and understanding. The Holy Spirit enables us to comprehend and apply these truths to our lives. The cycle continues when we choose to *live* according to what we have chosen to *believe*. We exercise our will when we choose to walk by faith and humbly submit to God. When we step out in faith, we grow in the knowledge of God, and we receive greater knowledge as we act on what we already know to be true. Strength, endurance, patience, joy, and thankfulness become increasingly evident in our character as we spiral upward.

We can block the growth process between any of the four points in the diagram. At the first stage (between knowledge and understanding), we can stop the process if we read the Bible as an academic exercise but never apply it to our lives. Doing so gives us intellectual knowledge but no spiritual wisdom or personal understanding of how God's Word transforms our lives. At the second stage (between wisdom and living it out), we can stop the process if we don't actually repent of the sin for which God has convicted us, or if we fail to act out on the direction God has provided. At the third stage, we can stop the process if we fail to deepen our relationship with God.

Finally, we can stop the growth process by failing to come back to God's Word gaining more knowledge of God's will. Paul addresses this problem when he wrote in Philippians 3:13–14, "Brothers and sisters, I do not consider myself yet to have taken hold of [the goal]. But one thing I do: Forgetting what is behind and straining toward what is ahead, I press on toward the goal to win the prize."

Review Colossians 1:9–14. What was Paul's prayer for the Colossian believers?

What are the four stages Paul outlines in the growth of a believer?

If the ultimate goal is to know God, why is it necessary to work through this cycle of growth?

As you look at the cycle of growth, which stage have you found most difficult to appropriate in your life?

How has knowing God's Word and living it out drawn you closer to God?

_____

_____

_____

Let us press onward and labor, watching with our whole heart. Let us be steadfast with all endurance; let us keep the Lord's commandments. Thereby, when that day of anger and vengeance comes, we may not be punished with the ungodly and the sinners. Rather, we may be honored with the righteous and with those who fear God.

Cyprian (AD 200–258)

Assurance of Salvation

God wants His children to be assured of their salvation. "I write these things to you who believe in the name of the Son of God so that you may know that you have eternal life" (1 John 5:13). Essentially, there are three means by which we can be assured of our salvation. The first is the witness of Scripture. God has taken the initiative to provide for our salvation, established the criteria by which we can experience it, and revealed the plan for both in His authoritative Word.

God secured our salvation by sacrificing His only Son to die in our place for our sins. Then, by His power, God resurrected Christ in order that we may have eternal life in Him. The means by which we can experience salvation is by believing in the finished work of Christ. "Everyone who believes that Jesus is the Christ is born of God" (verse 1). We are not saved by how we behave; we are saved by how we believe. Saving faith, however, is not just giving mental assent to what one chooses to believe.

Saving faith is relying on the death and resurrection of Christ as the only means for salvation.

The apostle Paul wrote, "If you declare with your mouth, 'Jesus is Lord,' and believe in your heart that God raised him from the dead, you will be saved. For it is with your heart that you believe and are justified, and it is with your mouth that you profess your faith and are saved" (Romans 10:9–10). We can mentally acknowledge that a historical person named Jesus died for our sins and rose again and not be born again. Believing that Jesus is Lord is not the same as believing that Jesus is "my Lord." Jesus is the Savior, but those who are saved confess Jesus as the Lord of their lives and live accordingly. What we choose to believe affects our walk and our talk, and if it doesn't, we really don't believe.

The second means by which we can be assured of our salvation is the internal witness of the Holy Spirit. Only God has the authority to confirm our status before Him, and He does for true believers. "The Spirit himself testifies with our spirit that we are God's children" (Romans 8:16). Our human spirit is in union with God when we are born again, providing confirmation that we are indeed children of God. "Because you are his sons, God sent the Spirit of his Son into our hearts, the Spirit who calls out 'Abba, Father'" (Galatians 4:6).

This inner witness is far more than a subjective feeling. The presence of the Holy Spirit in our lives brings a new love for God and a progressive detachment from the sinful attractions of this world. "For everyone born of God overcomes the world" (1 John 5:4). The true believer cannot continue in sin without being convicted by the Holy Spirit. Those who are struggling to overcome the entrapment of sin often question their salvation, but the very fact that their sinful behavior bothers them may be the best evidence that they are born again. The Holy Spirit will not take up residence in our lives and silently sit by while we continue to defile the temple of God. Christians who continue to live in sin are miserable, and they hate the sin that holds them in bondage.

The presence of the Holy Spirit also brings a new desire to read God's Word, along with the ability to understand it. "The person without the Spirit does not accept the things that come from the Spirit of God but considers them foolishness, and cannot understand them because they are discerned only through the Spirit" (1 Corinthians 2:14). The Holy Spirit is the Spirit of truth (see John 14:17), and "He will guide you into all truth" (John 16:13). That truth will confirm your status with your heavenly Father and set you free (see John 8:32). "Those who are led by the Spirit of God are the children of God" (Romans 8:14).

The external evidence of a changed life is the third assurance of our new life in Christ. New life in Christ brings a definitive change at the very core of our being, and this becomes evident in the way we think, feel, and behave. Our desires change and our language begins to clean up. Others begin to sense a difference in our demeanor as well as our behavior. John says, "Anyone who does what is good is from God. Anyone who does what is evil has not seen God" (3 John 1:11). James wrote, "What good is it, my brothers and sisters, if someone claims to have faith but has no deeds?" (James 2:14). We are saved by faith, but "faith by itself, if it is not accompanied by action, is dead. . . . Show me your faith without deeds, and I will show you my faith by my deeds" (verses 17–18). James is not challenging the doctrine of justification by faith. He is simply saying that if we really believe God and trust Him for our salvation, it will affect our walk and our talk.

The Story of God

The clay pots were forgiven, given new life, and set free to become like the Potter, but who is this Potter? Some pots had believed they were just part of an evolutionary process who had risen from the dust of the ground to their present form—an accident of nature. This no longer made sense to them, because nature when left to itself would revert to a lesser and more chaotic form of existence, not a greater and more ordered form. With this new life they were on an upward spiral of growth. It was like they were being compelled by a power greater than themselves. It was no easy transition from being the master of their own fate and the captain of their own soul to trusting someone other than themselves for their ultimate destiny.

When they started to read the Potter's instruction manual, they were surprised to find that they had been known from the beginning of time. The fact that they were known means there is an intelligence far greater than their own, and that intelligence is personal. Is it possible to actually know this Potter and have a personal relationship with Him? What's He like? Can they trust Him? Are His ways better than their ways? Knowing they couldn't become what the Potter wanted them to be by their own strength and resources, what attributes does He possess that will enable them to forge forward? The wise ones decided that the first order of business was to acquire a greater knowledge of the One who created them.

Daily Readings

Knowing God	Philippians 3:1–14
The Glory of God	Psalm 99:1–9
The Omnipresent God	Psalm 139:3–12
The Omnipotent God	Revelation 19:1–16
The Omniscient God	1 Chronicles 28:1–10

1

Knowing God

Philippians 3:1–14

Key Point

Although God is infinite and beyond our understanding, He has chosen to make Himself known to us through Christ.

Key Verse

I consider everything a loss because of the surpassing worth of knowing Christ Jesus my Lord, for whose sake I have lost all things.

Philippians 3:8

If anybody could qualify to have a relationship with God on the basis of the Old Covenant and their Jewish heritage, Paul would be the leading candidate. He was a "Hebrew of Hebrews" (Philippians 3:5), and "as for righteousness based on the law, faultless" (verse 6). Paul was a zealous defender of the faith and knew all about God, but until the Lord struck him down on the Damascus road, he didn't know Him at all. He had an Old Covenant relationship with God but not a personal one. After his conversion, Paul reflects on his lost status in the Jewish community: "But whatever were gains to me I now consider loss for the sake of Christ. What is more, I consider everything a loss because of the surpassing worth of knowing Christ Jesus my Lord, for whose sake I have lost all things" (verses 7–8).

The most important belief that we can have is a true knowledge of God and who we are in relationship to Him. Who is God? The Westminster Confession says, "God is a Spirit, infinite, eternal, and unchanging in His being, wisdom, power, holiness, justice, goodness and truth." Can we actually know Him? Scripture declares that God is incomprehensible. "How great is God—beyond our understanding! The number of his years is past finding out" (Job 36:26). Being finite we cannot fully comprehend the infinite, yet we can truly know Him. Paul prays "that the God of our Lord Jesus Christ, the glorious Father, may give you the Spirit of wisdom and revelation, so that you may know him better" (Ephesians 1:17).

God has made Himself known through His Word, but the written Word by itself can only give us a theology about God. The ultimate revelation of God is Jesus, His Son. Jesus said, "Anyone who has seen me has seen the Father" (John 14:9). It is through Christ that we personally know our heavenly Father. "No one knows the Son except the Father, and no one knows the Father except the Son and those to whom the Son chooses to reveal him" (Matthew 11:27). The triune nature of God is fully revealed in our relationship as children of God with our heavenly Father. "No one has ever seen God; but if we love one another, God lives in us and his love is made complete in us. This is how we know that we live in him and he in us: He has given us of his Spirit" (1 John 4:12–13). Because we have a personal relationship with God, we know Him as Father, Son, and Holy Spirit.

As children of God, we can personally petition our heavenly Father (see Matthew 6:9–13), because there is only one mediator between God and men, and that is Jesus Christ (see 1 Timothy 2:5). "This is the confidence we have in approaching God: that if we ask anything according to his will, he hears us" (1 John 5:14). As our heavenly Father, He "disciplines us for our good, in order that we may share in his holiness" (Hebrews 12:10). God knows us better than we know ourselves (see Hebrews 4:12–13), and He has made the ultimate sacrifice in order that we may know Him and have a personal relationship with Him through Jesus Christ.

Review Philippians 3:1–14. How did Paul's goal change after converting from Judaism to Christianity?

_____

_____

_____

What should the story of Paul's transition from the Old Covenant to the New Covenant (i.e., from law to grace) impact us today?

_____

_____

_____

What is the difference between knowing God and knowing about God?

_____

_____

_____

How can we personally get to know God better?

_____

_____

_____

What difference does it make to you personally to know that Christianity is a relationship as opposed to a religious ritual?

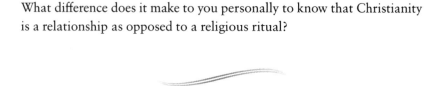

Consider what a great thing it was to restore the human form to people who had been turned to beasts. And without the law, there would be no grace. How so? Because the law served as a bridge. It was not possible to be raised from this extreme lowliness. So the law served as a ladder. Note that when a person has gone up a ladder, he no longer needs it. Yet he does not despise it, but gives it thanks, because it is due to the ladder that he is in the state of no longer needing it. . . . It is not the law that is a privation, but apostasy from Christ through adherence to the law. So when it leads us away from Christ it is a loss. When it leads us to him, no longer so.

John Chrysostom (AD 347–407)

2

The Glory of God

Psalm 99:1–9

Key Point

God is glorified when we manifest Him in our bodies by bearing much fruit.

Key Verse

Exalt the LORD our God, and worship at His holy hill; for the LORD our God is holy.

Psalm 99:9

God is holy, and no other attribute in the Bible speaks more directly to His deity. As the "Holy One" among us (Hosea 11:9), He is distinct and separate from all other things. He is "exalted over all the nations" (Psalm 99:2) and lives above and beyond all creation. The stain of sin and evil that defiled the world never had any effect on God. He has always been morally perfect and separate (or transcendent) from the rest of His fallen creation. As Isaiah writes, "The holy God will show Himself holy in righteousness" (Isaiah 5:16 NASB).

133

It is humanly impossible for us to grasp the glory of God, since no human being has ever fully seen Him. However, throughout the Bible we find individuals who were granted the privilege to witness a portion of His holiness. In Exodus 33:18, Moses said to God, "Show me your glory." The Lord responded by placing Moses in the cleft of a rock and allowing His glory to pass before him. God covered Moses' face, for "no one may see [God] and live" (verse 20). When Moses came down from the mountain, "his face was radiant" (34:29) from the glory of God, which slowly faded away.

Later, the prophet Isaiah was given a vision of God seated on a throne. Above Him, beings known as seraphim called out to one another, "Holy, holy, holy is the LORD Almighty; the whole earth is full of his glory" (Isaiah 6:3). When Isaiah realized God's holiness, he cried out, "Woe to me . . . I am ruined! For I am a man of unclean lips, and I live among a people of unclean lips, and my eyes have seen the King, the LORD Almighty" (verse 5). The prophet Ezekiel had a similar reaction when he received a vision of heaven. When he saw the Lord, he "fell facedown" (Ezekiel 1:28).

Our reaction would be the same if we were suddenly confronted with the glory of God. We see a clear example of this in the story of Jesus calling His first disciples. When a fisherman named Peter witnessed the power of Christ and realized who He was, he fell at Jesus' feet and said, "Go away from me, Lord; I am a sinful man!" (Luke 5:8). If we became more aware of God's glorious presence, the only sin we would be aware of is our own.

In the New Testament, believers are called to be sanctified (see John 17:19) and to be holy (see 1 Peter 1:16). The root word of "sanctification" and "holiness" is the same. As new creations in Christ, we have been set apart to live righteous lives. When we appreciate the glory of God, the gospel becomes even more amazing to us. As Paul said, "God from the beginning chose you for salvation through sanctification by the Spirit and belief in the truth, to which He called you by our gospel, for the obtaining of the glory of our Lord Jesus Christ" (2 Thessalonians 2:13–14 NKJV).

One day, when we have received a resurrected body, we shall be able to see God face to face with the acquired glory of our Lord Jesus Christ (see 1 John 3:2).

134

Review Psalm 99:1–9. How does the psalmist describe the way in which God is separate from His creation?

_____

_____

_____

_____

According to this passage, what are some of the ways that God revealed Himself to His people?

_____

_____

_____

Why did God tell Moses that no one could see His face and live?

_____

_____

_____

The Shekinah glory was a manifestation of God's presence, and we are called to glorify God in our bodies (see 1 Corinthians 6:20). How can we do that (see John 15:8)?

_____

_____

_____

How would our lives change if we did all to the glory of God (see 1 Corinthians 10:31)?

He cannot be seen—He is brighter than light. Nor can He be grasped—He is purer than touch. He cannot be estimated, for He is greater than all perceptions. He is infinite and immense. His greatness is known to Himself alone. But our heart is too limited to understand Him. . . . He who thinks he knows the magnitude of God is diminishing His magnitude.

Marcus Minucius Felix (c. late 2nd–early 3rd century AD)

3

The Omnipresent God

Psalm 139:3-12

Key Point

God is everywhere present and always near to those who call upon Him.

Key Verse

The heavens, even the highest heavens, cannot contain him.

2 Chronicles 2:6

The author of Hebrews writes, "In the beginning, Lord, you laid the foundations of the earth, and the heavens are the work of your hands" (Hebrews 1:10). God's story has no beginning and has no end. He is the Creator, not the creation, and while everything in the universe is present in one place in time, God is everywhere present (omnipresent) for all time. Solomon said of God, "Who is able to build a temple for him, since the heavens, even the highest heavens, cannot contain him?" (2 Chronicles 2:6).

God is not a tree or a rock, but He does sustain "all things by his powerful word" (Hebrews 1:3). If God ceased to exist, so would all creation, "for in him we live and move and have our being" (Acts 17:28). We cannot think of God as being in one place or another. David wrote, "If I go up to the heavens, you are there; if I make my bed in the depths, you are there. If I rise on the wings of the dawn, if I settle on the far side of the sea, even there your hand will guide me" (Psalm 139:8–10).

These are comforting words if we are seeking the security of His presence. On the other hand, if we—like Adam and Eve in the Garden—are trying to hide from Him, they can be threatening. The Bible is clear that it is impossible to flee from God. As the Lord said to the prophet Jeremiah, "Who can hide in secret places so that I cannot see them? . . . Do not I fill heaven and earth?" (Jeremiah 23:24). Even darkness cannot hide us from God, because darkness is as light to Him (see Psalm 139:11–12). Nor can the expanse of space set limits on Him, for He contains space itself.

Because God is everywhere present, He is "near to all who call on him" (Psalm 145:18). We may think of God as being remote from us, but that is not because He resides in some far-off galaxy. Rather, it is because of how different His nature is from our own. Sin has separated us from God in terms of relationship, and there is nothing we can do to reconnect with Him apart from the saving work of Christ.

God has promised, "Never will I leave you; never will I forsake you" (Hebrews 13:5). We should acknowledge His presence and increasingly become more aware of how He is working in our midst. It makes no sense to pray that God will "be with" us, since God, by His very nature, is always present. We should instead pray that God will enable us to become more conscious of His presence. David understood this when he wrote, "I have set the LORD continually before me; Because He is at my right hand, I will not be shaken" (Psalm 16:8 NASB).

We worship God when we ascribe to Him the divine attributes that only He possesses. The Lord doesn't need affirmation from us about who He is. He is fully secure within Himself. We worship God because we need to continually bring His divine attributes to our minds. We will never be alone as long as we acknowledge that our heavenly Father is always with us.

In Psalm 139:1–12, how does David acknowledge God's omnipresence?

What does David say about those who try to hide from God?

Why do some people feel that God is distant from them?

Does it comfort you to know that God is always present? Why or why not?

How can acknowledging the presence of God affect how you live?

This is the attribute of God, the Highest and Almighty, and the living God: not only to be everywhere present, but also to see all things and to hear all things. He is by no means to be confined in a place. For if He were, then the place containing Him would be greater than He. . . . For God is not contained, but is Himself the place of all.

Theophilus of Antioch (c. AD 163–181)

4

The Omnipotent God

Revelation 19:1–16

Key Point

God's power has no bounds except the limits He places on Himself due to His Word and His nature.

Key Verse

With man this is impossible, but with God all things are possible.

Matthew 19:26

Hallelujah! For our Lord God Almighty reigns" (Revelation 19:6). Such will be the praise of God's people in the final judgment when God has proven to everyone that He is "King of kings and Lord of Lords" (verse 16). The adjective "omnipotent" is rendered "Almighty" in Scripture and occurs only in the book of Revelation (see 1:8; 4:8; 11:17; 26:7, 14; 19:6, 15; 21:22), except for 2 Corinthians 6:18. God alone has the power to create something out of nothing. In addition to His original creation, the Bible records many "mighty acts" that no other created being can accomplish. He continues to express His power by creating new things (see Matthew 3:9; Romans 4:17) according to His pleasure, because nothing is too hard for God (see Genesis 18:14). In God resides the power to produce and control everything that comes to pass.

The power of God is demonstrated in His ability to ensure that all prophesies are fulfilled. To do that, God must have the ability to orchestrate whatever events are necessary in order for His Word to come true. This power is uniquely demonstrated in granting the barren Elizabeth to be pregnant with John the Baptist and impregnating the Virgin Mary so that Jesus could rightfully sit on the throne of David (see Luke 1:26–38). When the astonished Mary asked how this could be, "The angel answered, 'The Holy Spirit will come upon you, and the power of the Most High will overshadow you. . . . For nothing will be impossible with God'" (Luke 1:35, 37 NASB).

The omnipotence of God is only limited by His Word and nature because His power is of His own essence. For instance, God cannot lie (see Hebrews 6:18). God cannot be self-contradictory by sinning or dying. God cannot pretend that what has happened has not happened. God cannot use His power in an unwise or unholy way, and therefore He cannot abuse His power. Absolute authority corrupts absolutely for those who are corruptible, but God is incorruptible. God's omnipotence is controlled by His love.

Knowing the omnipotence of God is a tremendous blessing for the children of God. First, we are assured of His protection. "Whoever dwells in the shelter of the Most High will rest in the shadow of the Almighty. I will say of the LORD, 'He is my refuge and my fortress, my God, in whom I trust'" (Psalm 91:1–2). Second, "My God will meet all your needs according to the riches of his glory in Christ Jesus" (Philippians 4:19). Third, "I can do all this through him who gives me strength" (Philippians 4:13). It is incredible to think, but highly profitable to know, that God has extended His power to those who believe (see Ephesians 1:19). As believers, we don't have the power to do whatever we want; we have God's power to do His will. We can do everything through Christ that is consistent with His nature and will.

God is far more than an impersonal force that creates mountains and controls the forces of nature. He is the all-powerful God within us who lovingly uses His power to change us from sinners to saints. "For the message of the cross is foolishness to those who are perishing, but to us who are being saved it is the power of God" (1 Corinthians 1:18).

In Revelation 19:6 and 15, the word "omnipotent" is rendered "Almighty." How does John use these adjectives in this passage to describe the nature of God?

_____

_____

_____

_____

How does John depict God as the sovereign ruler of the universe?

_____

_____

_____

What would happen if God *didn't* set limits on His own power?

_____

_____

_____

What confidence do you draw from the fact that God's power has been extended to you when you believe?

_____

_____

_____

In what ways does God's power not entitle you to do all things, but rather enable you to be all that He created you to be?

_____

_____

_____

He is Lord, because He rules over the universe. He is Father, because He is before all things. He is Fashioner and Creator, because He is Creator and Maker of the universe. He is the highest, because He is above all. He is Almighty, because He Himself rules and embraces everything. The heights of heaven and the depths of the abysses, as well as the ends of the earth, are in His hand.

Theophilus of Antioch (c. AD 163–181)

5

The Omniscient God

1 Chronicles 28:1–10

Key Point

God participates with humanity in making legitimately free choices in such a way that God can know for certain the outcome.

Key Verse

As the heavens are higher than the earth, so are my ways higher than your ways and my thoughts than your thoughts.

Isaiah 55:9

Scripture clearly reveals that God is "all-knowing." "Great is our Lord and mighty in power; his understanding has no limit" (Psalm 147:5). He has perfect knowledge of the past (see Malachi 3:16) and of the future (see Isaiah 46:9–10). He knew us from eternity past (see Ephesians 2:10), and "for those God foreknew he also predestined to be conformed to the image of his Son" (Romans 8:29). It was because of God's omniscience that David admonished Solomon to serve God wholeheartedly, "For the LORD searches every heart and understands every desire and every thought"

(1 Chronicles 28:9). This truth is also taught in Hebrews 4:13: "Nothing in all creation is hidden from God's sight. Everything is uncovered and laid bare before the eyes of him to whom we must give account." Secret sin on earth is open scandal in heaven.

God's omnipresence partly explains His omniscience. Since He is everywhere present, His awareness is complete. Whereas mankind is bound by time, God is eternal. We understand the successive events of time and reason accordingly, but God sees the past, present, and future simultaneously. For God everything is "one eternal now." That which the finite mind sees in sequence is seen by God immediately in its totality.

It is impossible to know the future without having control over it. This creates a logical problem for the finite mind. How can Scripture teach both the sovereignty of God and the free will of humanity since we will be held accountable for the choices we make (see 2 Corinthians 5:10)? God's eternal knowledge of the future necessitates some degree of predetermination. In ways we cannot fully understand, God participates with humanity in making legitimately free choices in such a way that God can know for certain the outcome.

That God knows all things is clear from Scripture, but how He does know all things cannot be understood by us. "For my thoughts are not your thoughts, neither are your ways my ways, declares the LORD. As the heavens are higher than the earth, so are my ways higher than your ways and my thoughts than your thoughts" (Isaiah 55:8–9).

Francis Bacon said, "We cannot too often think there is a never-sleeping eye which reads the heart and registers our thoughts." People who live differently when they are alone than in the presence of others are usually ignorant that they are always living in full view of God. Knowing this truth about God could produce tremendous guilt if we didn't also know that "there is now no condemnation for those who are in Christ Jesus" (Romans 8:1). If you don't want God to know what you are thinking or doing, then don't think it or do it.

The omniscience of God is a tremendous blessing for believers. First, we can know that what God has said will certainly come to pass. Second, we can be led by the Holy Spirit, who knows the future. Third, we don't have to worry about tomorrow when our future is safely in the hands of God.

Read 1 Chronicles 28:1–10. What did God reveal to David about his son Solomon?

How is it possible that God can know our future when we have free will?

What security do believers receive in understanding that God is omniscient?

How does it make you feel knowing that "nothing in all creation is hidden from God's sight. Everything is uncovered and laid bare before the eyes of him to whom we must give account" (Hebrews 4:13)?

Knowing these things, how then should you live?

_____

_____

_____

God is both a perfect Father and a perfect Master. He is a father in His mercy, but a master in His discipline. He is a Father in the mildness of His power, but a master in its severity. He is a Father who must be loved with dutiful affection. Yet, He is a master who must be feared. He is to be loved, for He prefers mercy to sacrifice. Yet, he should be feared, because He dislikes sin. He should be loved, because He prefers the sinner's repentance over his death. Yet, he is to be feared for He dislikes the sinners who do not repent.

Tertullian (AD 160–220)

The Blessing

Since I am alive in Christ, by the grace of God:

I have been justified—completely forgiven (Romans 5:1).

I died with Christ and died to the power of sin's rule over my life (Romans 6:1–11).

I am free from condemnation (Romans 8:1).

I have been placed into Christ by God's doing (1 Corinthians 1:30).

I have received the Spirit of God that I might know the things freely given to me by God (1 Corinthians 2:12).

I have been given the mind of Christ (1 Corinthians 2:16).

I have been bought with a price; I am not my own; I belong to God (1 Corinthians 6:19–20).

I have been established, anointed, and sealed by God in Christ (2 Corinthians 1:21).

I have been given the Holy Spirit as a pledge guaranteeing my inheritance in Christ (Ephesians 1:13–14).

I have died with Christ and I no longer live for myself, but for Christ (2 Corinthians 5:14–15).

I have been crucified with Christ and it is no longer I who live, but Christ lives in me (Galatians 2:20).

I have been blessed with every spiritual blessing (Ephesians 1:3).

I was chosen in Christ before the foundation of the world to be holy and blameless before Him (Ephesians 1:4).

I was predestined—determined by God—to be adopted as God's son or daughter (Ephesians 1:5).

I have been redeemed and forgiven, and I am a recipient of His lavish grace (Ephesians 1:7).

I have been made alive together with Christ (Ephesians 2:5).

I have been raised up and seated with Christ in heaven (Ephesians 2:6).

I have direct access to God through the Spirit (Ephesians 2:18).

I may approach God with boldness, freedom, and confidence (Ephesians 3:12).

I have been rescued from the domain of Satan's rule and transferred to the kingdom of Christ (Colossians 1:13).

I have been redeemed and forgiven of all my sins (Colossians 1:14).

I have Christ within me (Colossians 1:27).

I am firmly rooted in Christ and am now being built up in Him (Colossians 2:7).

I have been spiritually circumcised (Colossians 2:11).

I have been made complete in Christ (Colossians 2:10).

I have been buried, raised, and made alive with Christ (Colossians 2:12–13).

I died with Christ and have been raised up with Christ. Christ is my life (Colossians 3:1–4).

I have been given a spirit of power, love, and self-discipline (2 Timothy 1:7).

I have been saved and set apart according to God's doing (2 Timothy 1:9; Titus 3:5).

I am being sanctified and made one with the Sanctifier (Hebrews 2:11).

I can come boldly before the throne of God to find mercy and grace (Hebrews 4:16).

I am a partaker of God's divine nature (2 Peter 1:4).

Leader's Tips

The following are some guidelines for leaders to follow when using the VICTORY SERIES studies with a small group. Generally, the ideal size for a group is between 10 and 20 people, which is small enough for meaningful fellowship but large enough for dynamic group interaction. It is typically best to stop opening up the group to members after the second session and invite them to join the next study after the six weeks are complete.

Structuring Your Time Together

For best results, ensure that all participants have a copy of the book. They should be encouraged to read the material and consider the questions and applications on their own before the group session. If participants have to miss a meeting, they should keep abreast of the study on their own. The group session reinforces what they learned and offers the valuable perspectives of others. Learning best takes place in the context of committed relationships, so do more than just share answers. Take the time to care and share with one another. You might want to use the first week to distribute material and give everyone a chance to tell others who they are.

If you discussed just one topic a week, it would take several years to finish the VICTORY SERIES. If you did five a week, it is possible to complete the whole series in 48 weeks. All the books in the series were written with a six-week study in mind. However, each group is different and each will have to discover its own pace. If too many participants come unprepared, you may have to read, or at least summarize, the text before discussing the questions and applications.

It would be great if this series was used for a church staff or Bible study at work and could be done one topic at a time, five days a week. However, most study groups will likely be meeting weekly. It is best to start with a time of sharing and prayer for one another. Start with the text or Bible passage for each topic and move to the discussion questions and application. Take time at the end to summarize what has been covered, and dismiss in prayer.

Group Dynamics

Getting a group of people actively involved in discussing critical issues of the Christian life is very rewarding. Not only does group interaction help to create interest, stimulate thinking, and encourage effective learning, but it is also vital for building quality relationships within the group. Only as people begin to share their thoughts and feelings will they begin to build bonds of friendship and support.

It is important to set some guidelines at the beginning of the study, as follows:

- There are no wrong questions.
- Everyone should feel free to share his or her ideas without recrimination.
- Focus on the issues and not on personalities.
- Try not to dominate the discussions or let others do so.
- Personal issues shared in the group must remain in the group.
- Avoid gossiping about others in or outside the group.
- Side issues should be diverted to the end of the class for those who wish to linger and discuss them further.
- Above all, help each other grow in Christ.

Some may find it difficult to share with others, and that is okay. It takes time to develop trust in any group. A leader can create a more open and sharing atmosphere by being appropriately vulnerable himself or herself. A good leader doesn't have all the answers and doesn't need to for this study. Some questions raised are extremely difficult to answer and have been puzzled over for years by educated believers. We will never have all the answers to every question in this age, but that does not preclude discussion over eternal matters. Hopefully, it will cause some to dig deeper.

Leading the Group

The following tips can be helpful in making group interaction a positive learning opportunity for everyone:

- When a question or comment is raised that is off the subject, suggest that you will bring it up again at the end of the class if anyone is still interested.

- When someone talks too much, direct a few questions specifically to other people, making sure not to put any shy people on the spot. Talk privately with the "dominator" and ask for cooperation in helping to draw out the quieter group members.

- Hopefully the participants have already written their answers to the discussion questions and will share that when asked. If most haven't come prepared, give them some time to personally reflect on what has been written and the questions asked.

- If someone asks a question that you don't know how to answer, admit it and move on. If the question calls for insight about personal experience, invite group members to comment. If the question requires specialized knowledge, offer to look for an answer before the next session. (Make sure to follow up the next session.)

- When group members disagree with you or each other, remind them that it is possible to disagree without becoming disagreeable. To help clarify the issues while maintaining a climate of mutual acceptance, encourage those on opposite sides to restate what they have heard the other person(s) saying about the issue. Then invite each side to evaluate how accurately they feel their position was presented. Ask group members to identify as many points as possible related to the topic on which both sides agree, and then lead the group in examining other Scriptures related to the topic, looking for common ground that they can all accept.

- Finally, urge group members to keep an open heart and mind and a willingness to continue loving one another while learning more about the topic at hand.

If the disagreement involves an issue on which your church has stated a position, be sure that stance is clearly and positively presented. This should be done not to squelch dissent but to ensure that there is no confusion over where your church stands.

Victory Series Scope
and Sequence Overview

The Victory Series is composed of eight studies that create a comprehensive discipleship course. Each study builds on the previous one and provides six sessions of material. These can be used by an individual or in a small group setting. There are leader's tips at the back of each study for those leading a small group.

The following scope and sequence overview gives a brief summary of the content of each of the eight studies in the Victory Series. Some studies also include articles related to the content of that study.

The Victory Series

Study 1   God's Story for You: Discover the Person God Created You to Be

---

Session One: The Story of Creation
Session Two: The Story of the Fall
Session Three: The Story of Salvation
Session Four: The Story of God's Sanctification
Session Five: The Story of God's Transforming Power
Session Six: The Story of God

Study 2   Your New Identity: A Transforming Union With God

Session One: A New Life "in Christ"
Session Two: A New Understanding of God's Character
Session Three: A New Understanding of God's Nature
Session Four: A New Relationship With God
Session Five: A New Humanity
Session Six: A New Beginning

Study 3   Your Foundation in Christ: Live by the Power of the Spirit

---

Session One: Liberating Truth
Session Two: The Nature of Faith
Session Three: Living Boldly
Session Four: Godly Relationships
Session Five: Freedom of Forgiveness
Session Six: Living by the Spirit

Study 4   Renewing Your Mind: Become More Like Christ

Session One: Being Transformed
Session Two: Living Under Grace
Session Three: Overcoming Anger
Session Four: Overcoming Anxiety
Session Five: Overcoming Depression
Session Six: Overcoming Losses

Coming Soon

Study 5   Growing in Christ: Deepen Your Relationship With Jesus

---

Session One: Spiritual Discernment
Session Two: Spiritual Gifts
Session Three: Growing Through Committed Relationships
Session Four: Overcoming Sexual Bondage
Session Five: Overcoming Chemical Addiction
Session Six: Suffering for Righteousness' Sake

Study 6   Your Life in Christ: Walk in Freedom by Faith

Session One: God's Will
Session Two: Faith Appraisal (Part 1)
Session Three: Faith Appraisal (Part 2)
Session Four: Spiritual Leadership
Session Five: Discipleship Counseling
Session Six: The Kingdom of God

Study 7 Your Authority in Christ: Overcoming the Enemy

Session One: The Origin of Evil
Session Two: God and Evil Spirits
Session Three: Overcoming the Opposition
Session Four: Kingdom Sovereignty
Session Five: The Armor of God (Part 1)
Session Six: The Armor of God (Part 2)

Study 8   Your Ultimate Victory: Standing Strong in the Faith

---

Session One: The Battle for Our Minds
Session Two: The Lure of Knowledge and Power
Session Three: Overcoming Temptation
Session Four: Overcoming Accusation
Session Five: Overcoming Deception
Session Six: Degrees of Spiritual Vulnerability

Books and Resources
Dr. Neil T. Anderson

Core Material

Victory Over the Darkness with study guide, audiobook, and DVD. With over 1,300,000 copies in print, this core book explains who you are in Christ, how to walk by faith in the power of the Holy Spirit, how to be transformed by the renewing of your mind, how to experience emotional freedom, and how to relate to one another in Christ.

The Bondage Breaker with study guide, audiobook, and DVD. With over 1,300,000 copies in print, this book explains spiritual warfare, what our protection is, ways that we are vulnerable, and how we can live a liberated life in Christ.

Breaking Through to Spiritual Maturity. This curriculum teaches the basic message of Freedom in Christ Ministries.

Discipleship Counseling with DVD. This book combines the concepts of discipleship and counseling and teaches the practical integration of theology and psychology for helping Christians resolve their personal and spiritual conflicts through repentance and faith in God.

Steps to Freedom in Christ and interactive video. This discipleship counseling tool helps Christians resolve their personal and spiritual conflicts through genuine repentance and faith in God.

Restored. This book is an expansion of the *Steps to Freedom in Christ*, and offers more explanation and illustrations.

Walking in Freedom. This book is a 21-day devotional that we use for follow-up after leading someone through the Steps to Freedom.

Freedom in Christ is a discipleship course for Sunday school classes and small groups. The course comes with a teacher's guide, a student guide, and a DVD covering 12 lessons and the Steps to Freedom in Christ. This course is designed to enable new and stagnant believers to resolve personal and spiritual conflicts and be established alive and free in Christ.

The Bondage Breaker DVD Experience is also a discipleship course for Sunday School classes and small groups. It is similar to the one above, but the lessons are 15 minutes instead of 30 minutes.

The Daily Discipler. This practical systematic theology is a culmination of all of Dr. Anderson's books covering the major doctrines of the Christian faith and the problems Christians face. It is a five-day-per-week, one-year study that will thoroughly ground believers in their faith.

Specialized Books

The Bondage Breaker, the Next Step. This book has several testimonies of people finding their freedom from all kinds of problems, with commentary by Dr. Anderson. It is an important learning tool for encouragers.

Overcoming Addictive Behavior, with Mike Quarles. This book explores the path to addiction and how a Christian can overcome addictive behaviors.

Overcoming Depression, with Joanne Anderson. This book explores the nature of depression, which is a body, soul, and spirit problem and presents a wholistic answer for overcoming this "common cold" of mental illness.

Liberating Prayer. This book helps believers understand the confusion in their minds when it comes time to pray, and why listening in prayer may be more important than talking.

Daily in Christ, with Joanne Anderson. This popular daily devotional is also being used by thousands of Internet subscribers every day.

Who I Am in Christ. In 36 short chapters, this book describes who you are in Christ and how He meets your deepest needs.

Freedom from Addiction, with Mike and Julia Quarles. Using Mike's testimony, this book explains the nature of chemical addictions and how to overcome them in Christ.

One Day at a Time, with Mike and Julia Quarles. This devotional helps those who struggle with addictive behaviors and explains how to discover the grace of God on a daily basis.

Freedom from Fear, with Rich Miller. This book explains anxiety disorders and how to overcome them.

Setting Your Church Free, with Charles Mylander. This book offers guidelines and encouragement for resolving seemingly impossible corporate conflicts in the church and also provides leaders with a primary means for church growth—releasing the power of God in the church.

Setting Your Marriage Free, with Dr. Charles Mylander. This book explains God's divine plan for marriage and the steps that couples can take to resolve their difficulties.

Christ-Centered Therapy, with Dr. Terry and Julie Zuehlke. This is a textbook explaining the practical integration of theology and psychology for professional counselors.

Getting Anger Under Control, with Rich Miller. This book explains the basis for anger and how to control it.

Grace that Breaks the Chains, with Rich Miller and Paul Travis. This book explains legalism and how to overcome it.

Winning the Battle Within. This book shares God's standards for sexual conduct, the path to sexual addiction, and how to overcome sexual strongholds.

The Path to Reconciliation. God has given the church the ministry of reconciliation. This book explains what that is and how it can be accomplished.

Rough Road to Freedom. This is a book of Dr. Anderson's memoirs.

For more information, contact Freedom In Christ Ministries at the following:

Canada: freedominchrist@sasktel.net or www.ficm.ca

India: isactara@vsnl.com

Switzerland: info@freiheitinchristus.ch or www.freiheitinchristus.ch

United Kingdom: info@ficm.org.uk or www.ficm.org.uk

United States: info@ficm.org or www.ficm.org

International: www.ficminternational.org

Dr. Anderson: www.discipleshipcounsel.com

Index

Dr. Neil T. Anderson was formerly the chairman of the Practical Theology Department at Talbot School of Theology. In 1989, he founded Freedom in Christ Ministries, which now has staff and offices in various countries around the world. He is currently on the Freedom in Christ Ministries International Board, which oversees this global ministry. For more information about Dr. Anderson and his ministry, visit his website at www.ficminternational.org.

Notes

Notes

Notes

Notes

Notes

Notes

Notes

Notes

Also From
Neil T. Anderson

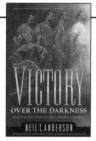

This bestselling landmark book gives you practical, productive ways to discover who you are in Christ. When you realize the power of your true identity, you can shed the burdens of your past, stand against evil influences, and become the person Christ empowers you to be.

Victory Over the Darkness

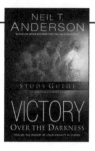

Great for small group or individual use, these thought-provoking personal reflection questions and applications for each chapter of *Victory Over the Darkness* will help readers grow in the strength and truth of their powerful identity in Jesus Christ.

Victory Over the Darkness Study Guide